WEST COAST TALES

Riveters, Wrecks and Ring-netters

Walter Weyndling

BIRLINN

To Gay,
who taught me to observe

First published in 2005
by Birlinn Limited
West Newington House
10 Newington Road
Edinburgh EH9 1QS

www.birlinn.co.uk

ISBN: 978 1 84158 346 4

British Library Cataloguing in Publication Data
A Catalogue record for this book is available from the British Library

Typesetting and origination by Brinnoven, Livingston
Printed and bound in the UK by CPI Antony Rowe, Chippenham and Eastbourne

CONTENTS

FOREWORD

No one of our generation had a better vantage point in our west of Scotland world of ships and boats than Walter Weyndling, and no one was more perceptive of what we were all up to. Walter's judgement on technical matters we all respected and accepted; here was a professional who combined his high qualifications with a practical and creative approach to problems. Walter applied the same constructive judgement, whether in interpreting new regulations for the largest of ocean-going ships, or checking the stern tube of an open boat in the Western Isles. Consideration was the hallmark of his professional dedication to ensuring that those going to sea had a well-found vessel.

Like a good physician with a broad practice, Walter knew us all well regardless of our role: tradesman, designer, skipper or executive. It is so very good that he could later look back on a world that has largely disappeared, and give to another generation an insight into the real world of ships, shipbuilding and boats that was inhabited by us old hands.

Walter always had a great enthusiasm for life and for service to his fellow human beings. He was of a people and a generation whose lives, if they had been spared, had been turned upside down. Our respect for him was redoubled by recognition of the ability that he chose to use in his own practical way, and without aggression among lesser men. Ours was a tough world of robust camaraderie tempered with the humour of our being all 'Jock Tamson's bairns'.

Friday was the day when Walter of the Board of Trade and the classification society surveyors lunched with the Lithgows' senior staff. My special memory does not concern a very large crude oil carrier, for Lithgows built the largest ships ever constructed in Great Britain, but the affairs of an associated company and a second-hand 'invasion' barge, which it was hoped could be used to link the island of Jura to Islay. The ferry then in use was an open boat for passengers only, enjoying the special 'island' classification, Class VI. But the barge proposed did not have the subdivision required for an enclosed boat, nor did she have the range of stability. Over coffee, these problems were solved on the tablecloth where buoyancy tanks were added and then Class VIa – an island open boat closed with a deck – was created. Board of Trade headquarters recognised the good practical sense of their surveyor extraordinary; Class VIa endures to this day.

Walter's work took him to the Islands and led to his becoming guide, philosopher and friend to those who plied their trade with boats there. He came to be held in affection by Highlanders as one of their own spirit. His life and that of his devoted wife Gay were always very full. Their work for the less fortunate filled much of the time that was left over from professional demands that were themselves accepted far beyond the call of duty. Their concern and work for others was unabated by 'exile' to the south, or retirement, or age, and they always kept in touch with those with whom they had been associated and become friends. I am sure that the readers of this book will capture something of this remarkable man as well as the world we used to work in.

W.J. Lithgow
Ormsary,
December 2004

PREFACE

I have been lucky to have had a home and to have worked for half of my life in Scotland, mostly on the West Coast. Here, I was even luckier to come across so many people and boats, to witness so many events and to have heard so many stories worth remembering – and to have enjoyed it all. My luck didn't end there – I have a wife who taught me to observe, and I was able to teach myself to listen.

The portrayal of some of the people I worked with may seem somewhat rose-tinted; that is because we became friends as I was doing my surveying.

What gave me perhaps the greatest pleasure was the enthusiasm with which these friends – fishermen, boatyard managers, skippers of ships big and small, ship designers, or these friends' widows or children – all thought it worthwhile to help me to record tales of their ships, their lives and their times. Co-authors of this book are legion and they are scattered mostly over the west of Scotland.

Much of the two chapters that tell of shipwrecks may seem technical and serious compared with the remainder of the book. Investigations of marine casualties took up a major part of my professional life. They were perhaps the most thought-demanding element of it – and I could not write light-heartedly of accidents in which sailors' lives were lost.

Walter Weyndling

Explanatory Note

My father died when the book was in the very last stages of preparation. He had planned to include an exhaustive list of acknowledgements to express his gratitude to the many people, on the West Coast and elsewhere, who gave so freely of their time and recollections, and without whom this book would have been so much the poorer.

Attempting to compile such a list now would be misguided. Too many names would inevitably be missed off. The book is therefore gratefully dedicated to the legion of co-authors that know who they are but must remain anonymous.

Richard Weyndling

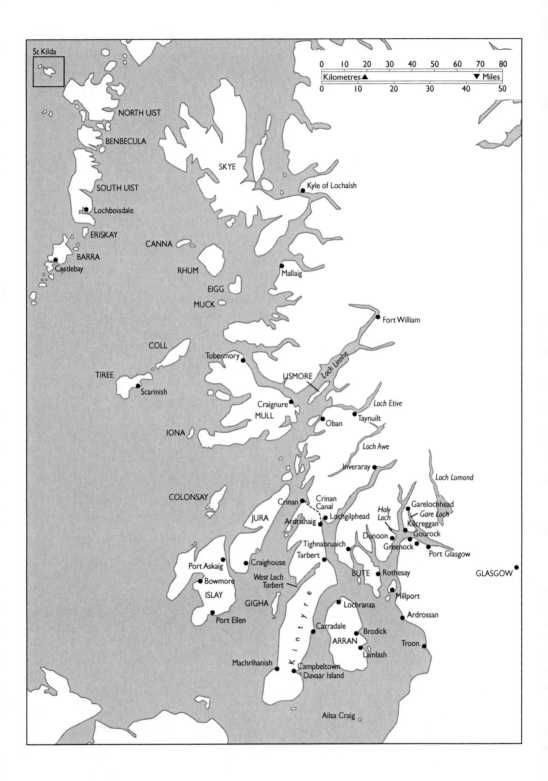

1
SHIPYARDS

Apprenticeship at Connell's

In the spring of 1940, I started my apprenticeship at Charles Connell's, a family owned and managed shipyard at Scotstoun in Glasgow. It was part of a 'sandwich course' in naval architecture at Glasgow University. My weekly wage was five shillings.

I was allocated to the drawing office, which had been resuscitated, along with the shipyard, only two or three years earlier, having been closed for several years during the depression. That was why the drawing office staff consisted only of apprentices and retired draughtsmen lured back 'for the duration' from retirement jobs, such as running a wee newsagent's or tobacconist's shop, or being a part-time bookmaker. The exception was Mr Alec Buchanan, the assistant chief draughtsman. The chief draughtsman's job was only half a job because it was, for a time, combined with that of a yard manager. He would come in at 8 a.m., spend an hour, or so, with the yard foremen and an hour, or so, going about the drawing office till about 11 a.m., when eighteen holes at golf could just be squeezed into the programme. Returning at 3 p.m. he would visit the yard and drawing office in reverse order.

I was the junior-most apprentice and my job for the first hour of each morning was making drawing ink, for which I was given a black and a red stick. The ink sticks were rubbed round wee, shallow dishes with a little water in each. When the inks were ready draughtsmen and apprentices queued to pick up their allocations. I spent the rest of my time tracing with ink plans drawn on transparent linen (which, when washed out, made high-class handkerchiefs for Sunday suits' breast pockets). Connell's shipyard employed no tracers, so tracing was shared between draughtsmen and apprentices. We were envious of the adjoining Barclay Curles yard, which employed swarms of young lady tracers, and at lunchtime we used to stand in wait outside Barclay Curles staff entrance in the hope of dating one of them.

1

Newly recruited apprentices used to be sent by draughtsmen to the yard on all kinds of traditional errands, such as asking for the key to the chain locker, starting with the foreman blacksmith. He would send one round all the other foremen. The chain locker was, of course, not a locker at all, but part of the forepeak which housed the anchor chain.

The apprentices would reciprocate by making abysmally silly epitaphs for the old gentlemen. Mr Wood was very ancient, so: 'Here lies the body of Mr Wood, if they hadn't pushed him over, he would still have stood'. Mr Cox had a long nose, so: 'Here lies the body of Mr Cox, they made a hole for his nose in the lid of his box'.

Getting back into town from Scotstoun called for a certain amount of ingenuity. All the city-bound tramcars used to rush past Scotstoun, mostly full of shipyard workers from the yards down the river – John Brown's, Yarrow's and Blythwood's. One of us had to take the courageous step of jumping on to the leading tramcar in slow motion. The conductress would scream, 'Come on. Get aff.', and threaten to call the driver to deal with the miscreant. While she was doing that, a number of not quite so full cars would have had to stop behind and we distributed ourselves amongst them. The offender would graciously leave the first car and jump on the last one just moving off.

In my second year of apprenticeship the drawing office had acquired wee Mr Burnett, a full-time chief draughtsman. He had a wee glass box from which to keep us under constant observation, and supervision became a lot stricter. Nobody was allowed to smoke in the drawing office except for old Mr MacNair, who had a doctor's 'line' which certified that smoking cheroots was part of his health treatment.

The shipyard was busy building a series of nearly identical 'tramp' ships and cargo-liners, which were in constant demand as replacements for Atlantic losses. I found the repetitive nature of the drawing office work rather boring, about the only exciting items of the plans to be traced were, for me, the exotic names of the various ranks and trades of the 'Lascar' (i.e. Indian seamen), such as 'serang', 'dhobi', etc.

Before long I asked for transfer to the shipwrights' department and was allocated to the 'mould loft' where the work was more rewarding. One of the principal tasks in the mould loft, which was not a loft at all but the floor of a huge shed, was the fairing of ship's lines. The transverse sections of a ship were condensed on a drawing known as the 'body plan', usually to the scale of half an inch to one foot. In the mould loft we marked each transverse section to full scale on a pitch pine floor and drew a long pliable wooden batten round the section, fixing it with sturdy nails known as 'dogs'. We looked along the curved batten and might find that the curve needed fairing by slicing a bit off here and slapping a bit on there. All this was done by eye and meant taking a dog or two out and allowing the wood batten to take up its natural spring. I used to think this process pretty satisfying.

A less sedentary task of the mould loftsman was to produce thin, yellow pine templates for all the curved plates of the ship's shell, which enabled the platers to cut the plates to the right dimensions and drill rivet holes in the right places. This involved taking measurements over the erected frames, i.e. the ship's bare skeleton, standing on a single plank for up to a height of fifteen feet, and on two planks above that height. The health and safety rules, if any, of those days were not as demanding as the present-day ones. Some of the other apprentices, sensing my insecurity at those heights, and probably from the best of motives, used to jump up and down on that single plank, to make me feel a wee bit more insecure.

We had no idea of geometrical development of three-dimensional curvatures until Jimmy Findlay came from John Brown's yard in Clydebank as assistant chief draughtsman and introduced us to a more scientific way of working. The chief loftsman, Jimmy MacAskill, an avuncular, rosy-cheeked native of the Outer Isles, in his seventies, could then be allowed to sit by the stove reading his *Sunday Post* and eventually to die 'in harness' because there was no pension scheme.

One had to be reasonably bright to qualify as a loftsman but the social mix of the loft reflected the general hearsay that Connell's was a 'convict yard'. It was said that Sir Charles' mother, a charitable lady, was a 'prison matron' and used to prevail on her husband to give ex-convicts a chance, and that tradition seemed to have persisted. Big Jock had done seven years in Peterhead and as a result could quote long passages from the Bible. Every Glasgow Fair week, the only annual shipyard holiday in those days apart from New Year's Day, Christmas not being a holiday, he used to send each of us a picture postcard of the guest house where he stayed in North Berwick with a cross against the window of his bedroom. Young Wully – I used to be known as Wally – had a habit of boasting of being a member of the Razor Gang. He did this with impunity, because his father was a 'polis'. Wee Jummy was from Duntocher and spoke the Duntocher variety of Clydeside speech. When asked 'Are you going to the pictures tonight?', he might respond 'No, I marny!' He once stuffed a wee coil of rope inside his jumper and tried to persuade the policeman

Girl welder

at the dock gate that it was 'stolen rope' and so qualify as another convict hero!

For all that, I never saw or experienced any violence while I was a shipyard apprentice. We all brewed our black tea in our black tins suspended at the ends of our individual sticks inside the boiler and exchanged sandwiches during short lunch breaks. Jummy used to complain nearly every day, 'Bloody cheese in my piece again'. In the end I asked him why he didn't ask his mum to put something else in his 'piece'. Jummy admitted grudgingly 'I make them myself'.

My apprenticeship was interrupted by my volunteering for aircrew in the RAF. It was the only way of getting out of a reserved occupation during the war, and one or two of my apprentice pals did it before me. A year later I was out of the RAF – where I wasn't a war hero but part aero-engine mechanic and part flight engineer – and destined for the Department of Naval Construction. While I was waiting for the Lords of the Admiralty to send for me, I tried to continue my shipyard apprenticeship, but was pronounced too old for it and was made, for a few months, a junior manager in charge of girl welders. Welding had just come in and in Connell's shipyard girls were welding prefabricated parts of LSTs (Landing Ships, Tanks). What conscientious and hard working welders most of them were!

Alexander Stephen and Son

A little more than a decade later I was back on the Clyde, this time as a Board of Trade ship surveyor and my domain was on the south side of the river. In the 1950s Alexander Stephen and Sons in Govan was amongst the upper strata of Clyde ship builders. One of the oldest Scottish family shipyards, it had started in Aberdeen in 1750 and moved to Linthouse in Glasgow in 1870. In my time Stephens were building a number of refrigerated cargo-liners for the P&O and Elders and Fyffes groups. The latter's 'banana ships' had high-class accommodation for a small number of passengers.

In that period of the 1950s Stephens embarked on a programme of modernisation. They were amongst the first to make a sizeable investment in electric mono-tower travelling cranes and in welding technology. As their order book diminished Stephens engaged a management consultant and acquired a 'productivity office' filled with bright young men and women plotting curves and sticking wee flags in them. Another brave step of that period was Stephens' absorption of the Simon-Lobnitz shipyard and the production of three self-propelled suction dredgers for the Soviet Union, which are still operating in Russia. In the late 1950s Stephens shared with Harland & Wolff an order for six medium-size BP tankers. Being in the avant-garde of technology, these tankers were amongst the first welded ships of any size.

Stephens' repair department was looking after some of the ships of the Brocklebank wing of the Cunard Group. They were mostly in the Indian trade and carried Indian crews. These ships, when in Stephens' yard, were specially popular with the surveyors as their Goanese cooks were renowned for their curry lunches.

The name of Stephen of Linthouse is now only a memory and half of its shipyard and engine works site is taken up by Barr & Stroud high-tech optical range-finder makers.

Harland and Wolff, Govan

Harland & Wolff's Charlie Simpson was a shipyard boss of the old style and there was not much evidence of modernisation about the place. It was a matter of considerable satisfaction to him that his all-riveted BP tankers were produced at a lower cost than the Stephens' welded ones.

Charlie was a true blue Rangers man and any visitor who happened to be so misguided as to display a green tie would be made aware in a more-or-less discreet whisper that he wouldn't be welcome in the directors' dining room. And in so doing he would miss seeing the extraordinary display of silver trophies and silverware donated by appreciative ship-owners.

In 1958 Harland & Wolff built *Tri-Ellis*, a ship designed to carry refrigerated cargo and passengers to, and phosphates from, Christmas Island, one of the Line Islands in the Pacific. On the day of her sea trials everyone involved in the building and testing of the ship, down to the author, was assembled on board for the decisive occasion. Finally the mooring ropes were let go and the ship moved off down the Clyde. Then the phone rang on the bridge, 'Mrs Weyndling has locked herself out of the house and would Mr Weyndling please come ashore to let her have his key!'

Between 1958 and 1961 Harland & Wolff Govan produced a most handsome batch of cargo-liners, the 'B' Class of motor ships for the

Glasgow 1960

British India Steam Navigation Company. With sloping sheer, elegantly raked bow and superstructure, futuristic looking deck cranes and angled integral radar mast and funnel they were prime candidates for the title of finest looking cargo liners built on the Clyde.

The Govan shipyard, acquired by the Belfast parent company only in 1912, previously bore the names of Robert Napier and William Beardmore, both significant in the nineteenth-century history of Scottish shipbuilding. It was distinctive among Clyde shipyards in being the farthest away from the open sea and in each of its six building berths having individual dock gates, which allowed work at all states of the tide. Closure came in 1963 although the concern was profitable at the time of closure. Most of the site is now taken up by council housing but one of the outfit sheds remains and is used as an industrial theatre.

Ardrossan Dockyard

The Ardrossan Dockyard, as I knew it, had been in existence for over a hundred years and had not enjoyed extensive investment in replacing historic plant and equipment. In spite of all this, with its small but adaptable labour force, it was kept busy on building smallish ships, ship repair and conversions. It was run by John Coleman, a charismatic Irish gentleman, whose philosophical outlook on life coloured his dealing with business associates. On one occasion I was prevailed upon to stay on after 5 p.m. so as to continue surveying a ship undergoing repair. In due course I received a message from Mr Coleman asking if I would like to join him for a quick cup of tea at the local hostelry before resuming work. I was ushered into a wee private section of the hotel bar and over a dram we struck up conversation, interrupted only slightly by the arrival of a pile of sandwiches. After the second dram the exchange of views became more meaningful and after the third one matters of real importance came under discussion. The continuation of the ship survey receded into murky distance . . . just as well it happened before the days of breathalysing.

In the early 1960s the ownership of the Ardrossan Dockyard changed hands and the new managing director was Archie Kelly, a Greenock entrepreneur, who made his fortune as a ship boiler and ship double-bottom cleaning contractor. Archie was affectionately known as 'Cash down' Kelly since he was reputed to have offered a cool million pounds cash for John Brown's shipyard when it first got into financial difficulties. He then got into the habit of buying up and selling – when enough money was offered – smaller Scottish and Irish shipyards. Once, over lunch at the Star Hotel in Port Glasgow, he offered me a directorship of the newly acquired Ardrossan Dockyard. I suppose that in the all-pervasive climate of liberal economics, it must have seemed unnatural for Crown servants to be unable to take up outside appointments of profit and to pay attention to such little things as conflicts of interest!

The dockyard lingered on repairing ships until 1969 when it was sold to Ardrossan Harbour Board for the extension of their ferry terminal.

Ferguson Brothers, Port Glasgow

Towards the end of the 1950s I moved from my Glasgow base and came to work out of Greenock and to become the 'necessary evil' for some shipyards in Port Glasgow and Greenock for nearly two decades.

Ferguson Brothers shipyard, located west of Newark Castle in Port Glasgow, was founded at the very beginning of the twentieth century, when four Ferguson brothers broke away from the Fleming & Ferguson Shipyard at Paisley. It was still very much a family business when I appeared on the scene. All the directors were Ferguson cousins, but not all Ferguson cousins were directors. The exception was unrelated Horace Hewson, a very pukkah-looking colonel who somehow succeeded in running the shipyard along army lines. It was only a few years earlier, when Old Peter Ferguson was in charge, that official functions were family affairs, almost like grandmother's birthdays. It was said that at a ship launch the platform party was invited to the boardroom to be treated to a glass of cream sherry and a slice of Dundee cake.

When I came along, old Peter's nephew Robert Ferguson was managing director with two cousins and a brother-in-law as co-directors. The shipyard did not become part of the Lithgow Group until 1963. In those early days amongst the bread and butter products of Newark Shipyard were coal-fired steam tugs for South African Railways. The steam engines were being built in one of the shipyard sheds, next to the platers' shed. Boilers had to be imported all the way from Greenock. Such tugs made sense for South Africa where both coal and labour were cheap and readily available.

Amongst the more memorable ships built in that period were two ferries for the Trinidad to Tobago crossing, *Bird of Paradise* and *Scarlet Ibis*. The first ferry captain to arrive in Port Glasgow was the personification of a Red Indian Chief, who to the delight of the romantically inclined ladies of Port Glasgow turned out to be a sociable and gentlemanly person. I remember vaguely a tumultuous commissioning party on board either one of those two ferries, or else on *Makouria*, a ferry for British Guiana. It would have lasted all night were it not for the revellers setting off the fire-fighting sprinkler system, which somewhat cooled their ardour.

The only West Coast passenger ferry built at Newark in my time was the *Sound of Islay* for Western Ferries. She was contracted on a fixed price basis and the cost of construction soon exceeded that amount, but the shipowners stuck to the contract figure. It so happened that at the time Sir William Lithgow was the principal shareholder in both Ferguson Brothers and Western Ferries. When asked by his shipbuilder co-directors how he proposed to get out of the impasse he was reputed to have replied 'Sue the b——s!'

One of the later specialities of Ferguson's shipyard's output was dredgers. Some designs were quite sophisticated. One such was a variable density suction dredger suitable for both gravel and sand. The associated calculations became so involved that the shipyard director and naval architect proposed that he and I have a meeting with Jimmy, the principal surveyor concerned at the Board of Trade London headquarters. The great man greeted us affably and opened up with small talk about one's holidays. He went on in colourful detail about the hardships of having a villa in the south of Spain and in particular about the problems of maintaining a swimming pool there. Midday came and, as we were expressing our sympathy over his troubles, he suddenly remembered that he was due at a lunch appointment. He effusively bid us goodbye and, with a wave of hand towards me, indicated that should there be any matters needing clarification the senior ship surveyor in Greenock would be more than capable of coping with it.

Some of the trawlers built at the Newark yard were for the Scottish and English Departments of Agriculture and Fisheries and some for Hull owners. The departmental orders were for research vessels, which some suspected were also used for intelligence gathering. This, by conjecture, may have been instrumental in creating suspicion that the lost trawler *Gaul*, of the same owners, along with some from Ferguson's, could have been involved in spying. Everyone got so used to the research trawlers, with their elaborate aerials, undergoing prolonged trials in the Firth that when a Russian trawler of similar silhouette nonchalantly sailed into the Gareloch, no one cottoned on to the fact that it wasn't one of the UK research vessels!

Just about the last ship to come out of Ferguson's before my departure was the *Gardeloo*, a sludge carrier for Midlothian County. She also performed nobly as a comfortable and hospitable seabird watchers' carrier. The only time the 'twitcher' passengers were advised to seek shelter below deck was when *Gardeloo* was discharging her cargo at Bell Rock.

I remember the Newark shipyard in the late 1950s and early 1960s was a traditional establishment with wood scaffolding, and bowler hats distinguishing managers and foremen. Somehow the few carpenters from St Kilda, working there at the time, added to the old-fashioned feeling about the place. They had been evacuated from that island more than twenty years earlier, but old habits die hard. I watched one of them climbing all the way down from deck-high scaffolding to pick up a nail he'd dropped.

Riveting of ships' plates went on at the Ferguson's yard till the early 1960s. I met there, on the whole, a superior quality of workmanship, rivet holes in plates being mostly drilled rather than punched. By the mid-1960s the younger riveters were being retrained as welders as the older ones were retiring. When in 1966 two riveted hopper barges were being built for South Africa, the retrained riveters could call their own price for reverting to their old trade, and a taxi had to be sent round to extricate retired riveters from their armchairs.

When checking the quality of riveting in the ship's tanks and double bottom I used to be accompanied by a 'searcher', usually Dick Devenish, a semi-retired riveter, a character and a man of much experience. From time to time we would stop for a fag; unbelievable today, we enjoyed having a smoke in a tight corner of a very tight and stuffy space. In such a situation one was inclined to talk of anything rather than the day's business of rivet tapping. There could be an odd occasion for name dropping and the names dropped by Dick, more often than not, referred to a lecturer cousin or a headmaster nephew. This was not untypical of the academic aspirations of the tradesmen, or rather craftsmen, of the Clyde.

By the time I was leaving the Clyde, in the later 1970s, Ferguson Brothers had become the most up-to-date of the remaining Scottish shipyards. Not only had their design become computerised, but so had the means of translating the design into units of steel construction, taking the place of the old mould loft. The shipyard is going strong at the time of writing and is not only in the forefront of naval architecture technology, but it has returned to annual profits, partly thanks to timely completion of contracts and to share ownership by the labour force.

Lamont's of Greenock

Lamont's ship repair yard at Dock Breast in Greenock and the adjacent, leased East India dry-dock were where nearly all the MacBrayne, Caledonian Steamship Company and later CalMac ships came for annual dry-docking and overhaul. At the head of that establishment stood wee Bertie, a rotund gentleman with a good sense of humour and a well-rooted suspicion of all surveyors. This sentiment was reciprocated by surveyors

In the course of a dry-docking survey the surveyor tapped every rivet of the hull repair and then demanded the compartment be tested with a head of water, if possible. The simplest way of checking that a head of water had been pressed on the compartment was to find water in the air-pipes serving that compartment before examining each rivet of the riveted hull repair for leakage. I don't know what made me look inside the tank just tested, after water had been drained out of it. It was then I noticed wooden plugs in each of the air-pipe apertures in the deck. One of Bertie's under-managers had saved himself the trouble of filling that tank by just filling the air-pipes.

Bertie, on the other hand, seemed to be convinced that all surveyors and ship superintendents were in league in some sort of conspiracy against Lamont's and that the clever policy was to try to divide them, by making them suspicious of each other. Apart from these conspiratorial machinations there were a number of distractions that tended to occur in the Lamont's surveyors' and superintendents' changing room. One such could be expected with the arrival there of Mr Graham, the engineer superintendent of the Calor gas carrying fleet owned by Capt. Cunningham of Scalpay, Harris. Known as 'Hurricane' Graham because of his gentlemanly attitude to unnecessary expedition, he was always accompanied by his mathematical dog. We were expected to be an audience for the show and did not dare start work before it had taken place. An increasing number of wooden markers from one to five were put in front of the canine performer and he barked the appropriate number of times.

One of the odd craft encountered at Lamont's yard that comes to mind, was *Arno*. She was a wartime landing craft bought by a Spanish company undertaking oil exploration on the stretch of African west coast then known as the Spanish Sahara. I carried out a survey for the issue of a load line certificate for *Arno*'s voyage with not a little difficulty as none of the crew, apart from the captain, had a word of English. After

The *Arno*

weeks of persevering toil *Arno* was ready to head southwards. That she didn't leave on the appointed day was because her crew refused to go to sea without a supply of *bacalhao*, which means strips of cod sun-dried at sea off Newfoundland Banks. The matter was only resolved when my wife, having cruised around Glasgow in search of the delicacy, eventually found a supply in a wee Italian shop in Shawlands.

George Brown's Garvel Yard

The Garvel shipyard of George Brown was situated at the northern point of an artificial island created between the Clyde, James Watt Dock and the Great Harbour at Greenock. It was known in common Greenock parlance of the past as 'Klondyke', because men did so well working there in the First World War. The later, less affectionate nicknames of 'Siberia' or 'Stalingrad' referred to the shipyard's exposure to north-easterly winds.

I recall the little Garvel yard in the 1960s and 1970s as being a happy family concern, one Brown brother acting as shipyard manager, another as general manager and a son as naval architect. They were a family of enterprising and innovative shipbuilders, engineers and naval architects, capable of retaining a small, contented labour force for most the yard's existence. Browns designed and built a variety of steel craft ranging from a coastal tanker to trawlers, in response to fluctuating demand. To ensure continuity of employment they founded a successful company under the name of Cargo-speed to design and manufacture, on the site, a variety of ship equipment such as derricks, ship cranes, bow and stern doors. The firm ceased trading in the 1980s largely due to the international competition becoming too aggressive for a small concern.

Life in Port Glasgow

Port Glasgow of the 1950s, '60s and '70s was a fairly homogeneous and closely knit community; no West and East Ends; the shipyard manager and the shipyard gateman living cheek by jowl on one of the hillside terraces such as the Ivy Bank or Lily Bank. If there was a class distinction it was perhaps between the apprenticeship served craftsmen and the semi-skilled or unskilled men. The style of life of craftsmen and their educational aspirations were perhaps more akin to those of the middle class than those of what was loosely called the working class. I knew platers whose sons qualified to become draughtsmen and whose sons' sons qualified to become managers.

Such class distinction as there was usually, but not always, coincided with the difference of church allegiance. The shipwrights, the platers and the riveters were more likely to attend the Church of Scotland or the Scottish Episcopal Church and their 'mates' the Roman Catholic Church. To define the term 'mates' I have to recall the old shipyard practice of squads that would undertake to deliver a portion of the ship's hull, such as a bulkhead, for a price. A squad might consist of a shipwright and a number of platers, riveters and mates or semi-skilled or unskilled assistants. The payment for the 'job' would usually be divided among members of the squad according to seniority, but sometimes, unofficially, according to each member's number of children. The importance of some of the crafts was diminished with the introduction of welding in the late 1950s and early '60s. It needed craftsmen, platers and riveters to produce a satisfactory joint of three riveted plates but welding them was relatively straightforward.

Lithgow Shipyards

The year 1962 was the 150th anniversary of the launching in Port Glasgow of the world's first sea-going steamship for which the local industry had built a replica, complete with engine copied from the original in the Science Museum. Before a commemorative voyage with suitably attired dignitaries could be made to Helensburgh, the original's home port, it fell to me to certify the vessel seaworthy. I was able to dispense with the need for certain trials as this was a duplicate of a proven class of ship!

Before departing from the Newark end of Port Glasgow a little may be said about the company which assembled for lunch, at least once a week, at the Star Hotel there. Round the table I might meet John Peach of Ferguson Brothers, Donald Main, the Procurator Fiscal and a raconteur, one or two other local notables and Willie Wilson, a plumbing contractor to the shipyards. Willie, a likeable chap, was not always aware of the world around him. Sometimes he was late coming to lunch, delayed by his car having had a brush with another car, usually due to the other chap's car door handle or wing mirror sticking out too far. On one occasion Willie came in quite sorry for himself. Calling on the local Boots he had walked into a glass door, knocked out, treated to a little brandy to revive him in the shop, and was promptly apprehended for being in charge of a car under the influence of alcohol. Once, as I was parking in Lithgow's car park, Willie arrived in his car waving to me in his usual friendly fashion and I made space for him to park alongside. To my consternation he walked away oblivious to having made it impossible for me to get out of my car! I had to hoot for someone to open my hatchback and allow me to crawl out that way.

I came to be associated with Lithgow shipyards in the 1950s when Sir William Lithgow was a young man, not long out of his teens, and his mother, a lady of great charm and dignity, still the company chairman. His father died when he was still a teenager and left him not only a clutch of shipyards and assorted engineering enterprises but a title and a substantial fortune. A story still went around in my days that young William taking his first walk through the yard after his father's death was addressed by one of the yard labourers, 'Awfy sorry aboot yer faither, Sir William. Could you lend me a million till Friday?' I used to meet young William at Friday boardroom lunches when he was always bursting with new ideas. I also remember being introduced to his glamorous new young wife Mary Claire at a sherry party. She said something pleasant to me but

Aerial view of Lithgow's yards

never got an answer. I had been inadvisedly taking a bite of a biscuit and had broken a front tooth as she was speaking to me!

In the two main Lithgow shipyards in Port Glasgow the manpower differed also along the lines of church allegiance. The largest and most modern Kingston Yard was manned almost entirely by Protestants; and the East Yard by Catholics up to charge hand level. While the Kingston Yard was building mainly bulk carriers and tankers, the East Yard built also a number of cargo-liners for Paddie Henderson, known for providing a service to Burma second only to Bibby Line. The third of the Lithgow shipyards in Port Glasgow, known as the Hamilton Yard, was in my time building a number of ships for Elder Dempster Lines who were famed for the regiment of superintendents standing by their ships under construction. One who particularly comes to mind was the aptly named Mr Bucket, the plumbing superintendent. Hamilton Yard offices were located on three floors of a tenement in Port Glasgow, known as Miramishi building. Dr Weir's surgery was on the ground floor, Murray's pub was at one time also on the ground floor, or next door, or almost next door.

After East Yard ceased production in 1969/70, Hamilton Yard, renamed Glen Yard, was endowed with a 900 ft building berth suitable for tankers of about 150,000 tons, or of larger deadweight using two part construction.

Kingston Yard was the hub of the Lithgow's shipbuilding domain in Port Glasgow, at the time producing a ship a month on the average. The hub of the hub was the design office, at the head of which stood Hugh Currie, the naval architect and later general manager and director of Lithgow's, leading a lively team of young designers such as Willie Ferguson, Tommy Dean and others, and of his contemporaries such as Harry Duncan. He shone in his profession and will be remembered, amongst other things, for his idea of the ram bow, which reduced the resistance to motion of the bulk carriers. A man of natural charm and sense of humour, he succeeded in being a leader of men while remaining one of them. Hugh became the chairman of the Greenock Morton Football Club whose fortunes measured the enthusiasm of the Lithgow workforce and so related to the shipyard's productivity. In April 1974 Hugh and I were in Lisbon in connection with dry-docking of the Lithgow's supertanker there. We were caught up by the bloodless revolution of 25 April, which swept from power the regime of Salazar's successors. With the dry-dock and the Lithgow's small expeditionary workforce being immobilised by those events, we had time to wander through the red-bannered city. At one point we observed in a cavalcade of motorcycles a substantial lady rider decked out in red ribbons and flowers shouting, 'Viva a Liberdade!' Clinging behind her, on a pillion, was a wee Lithgow's shipyard welder calling 'Up Greenock Morton!'

Hugh was promoted to general manager and director at the age of forty. This was considered a momentous event for a man who started from a drawing board and got his qualifications at a night school, and it caused him to be besieged by the press. It was, I think, a reporter from *Lloyds List* who asked Hugh to name some of the institutions he was a member of. Hugh scratched his head and said the only one he could think of was the Port Glasgow Cooperative. His wife Jean interjected: 'He is boasting. It is me who is the Co-op member.'

The calculating part of the Lithgow's design office was housed in a wee glass enclosure within which Harry Thomas reigned supreme. Old Harry, tall, gaunt and somewhat lame, was a very north country Englishman who fetched up in the west of Scotland by some freak of economic ebb and flow. He was old fashioned in every sense of that adjective, and used to reminisce on the wonders of the pre-war English north country seaside resorts – tales of such exhibits as the Vicar of Stiffkey, the bearded lady and the double-headed sheep. And yet Harry was adept not only at the use of the barrel slide rule for ship calculations

Ross Belch, Hugh Currie & Neil Mackay

but took the computer generation of ships' hydrostatic and stability cross-curves in his stride.

The temperature in the design and calculating offices of Lithgow's used to rise, sometimes to fever point, towards the end of each ship contract and that, for obvious reasons, engulfed myself. Getting all the certificates signed and in place, having the stability books approved for various bulk cargoes, including grain, for some reason used to coincide with new rules being promulgated, final tests and trials! We all breathed with relief when each ship, fully equipped and documented, sailed past Cloch Lighthouse, on her way 'doon the wa'er'.

During my association with Lithgow's the 'high heid yin's' job was passed on from Alec White, of the old school of shipyard management concentrating on keeping the business on an even keel, to the exuberant Ross Belch, general manager and director since the 1950s. I had known Ross since our student days at Glasgow University and already then he was showing his capacity for acting in several leading roles at once. This used to leave little time for other, more or less important, functions of everyday life. And so near midnight Ross would blow into a study of the Maclay Hall students' residence, just as others were winding up their studies, having put to rights one or another of the university organisations he chaired. Hence, in the morning he had so little time in the communal bathroom that sometimes he had to borrow a shaving brush from one of his friends and a toothbrush from another. Later he could be seen running down Kelvin Park towards Gilmore hill with a cup of tea in one hand and toast and marmalade in another. All this didn't prevent him from graduating with first class honours in naval architecture.

The 'late' Ross Belch, still in breathless pursuit of time, turned out to be a remarkable manager of men in his single-minded striving for the greater glory of the Lithgow shipbuilding dominion. The shipyard managers were in some way his extended family, which he gathered, with their wives, some weekends in his Murray Park hotel at Crieff to share with them his plans for the firm's future. This was colloquially referred to as 'Ross's Sunday School'. Unlike some other shipyard managers, Ross treated all Lithgow men on equal terms and had such a way with them that stories were told of people who came in to ask him for a rise and came out thanking him for not getting one. And all the time his concentration on Lithgow business was such that when one was sitting beside him at dinner his notepad was never far away and notes were taken of any crumbs of information that might be useful to the shipyards and to himself. One of his staff told me how he once looked over his shoulder and caught sight of this entry in his notebook, 'Cut nails'. To try and complete the list of his fortes, Ross excelled as a conciliator, a skill came in handy when negotiating with the unions.

One of the best Belch stories was told by his first wife Jan, who sadly died quite young. In the wave of democratisation that followed Ross's appointment as Lithgow managing director there was a move to win over the shop floor. Part of this process was a series of dances in the Lithgow club to which all levels of management, all shop stewards and their wives were invited. The bar was kept fairly busy. Jan told how halfway through the evening she was asked to dance by one of the stewards, who almost at once started to chat her up. He said, 'You're a nice wee lassie – I like you.' Jan replied, 'I like you too.' Said the steward, 'Whit's yer name?' to which Jan replied, 'Mrs Belch'. At which point the steward gave a strangled cry of, 'Oh, my Goad!' and dropped her more or less in mid-pirouette in the centre of the dance floor. So much for democracy!

Neil Mackay, of Islay sea-going stock, was nominally the Lithgow office manager but was in fact known as 'Mr Fix-it'. He was probably the most useful man to know at Lithgow's. One of his many jobs was to organise events and to make sure that invitations went to the right places. The Glasgow airport manager was a must. Neil had to be able to phone him and ask him to hold the London plane because 'Mr Belch was just on his way'. I can remember only one occasion when Neil's organisation did not come up to scratch. He couldn't get up-market caterers for the important lunch at the Greenock Town Hall following one of Clarkson's ship's launches. The food was barely passable and the drink virtually non-existent. Sandy Glen, speaking as chairman of Clarkson's, started off, 'Can I first propose a toast to absent friends, with which I would like to couple the name of the wine waiter.' He got the biggest cheer of the day.

The Caledonia Joinery Company was a semi-autonomous member of the large Lithgow brotherhood, run efficiently and profitably and yet humanly by George Anderson and Willie Creighton, the managing director and manager respectively. They were both active Christians and directed the enterprise on those lines, an example being their apprenticeship scheme in which boys from poorer backgrounds were given a helping hand. I was puzzled as to why George was often referred by his men as 'Cadona' which was the name of a Scots/Italian family who used to run the annual 'shows'. At last a joiner told me, 'Every time he's grumpin oan at you aboot somethin' he keeps saying "yez a' ken ah'm a fair man"'.

I remember some wee and not so wee kindnesses discreetly directed by George or Willie at less needy recipients. One such was Archie Macphee, the Port Askaig ferryman, and a client of mine, who badly wanted a piece of joinery material he could not come by on Islay. A whisper into a receptive ear resulted in that object finding itself on the lorry carrying some furniture to Sir William Lithgow's home at Ormsary. The lorry happened to be passing the Islay ferry pier at Kennacraig and happened to drop 'the thing' at the pier, from where it happened to be thrown on board by the ferry crew.

During the one and only joiners' strike I can remember Willie asked me if I could think of some way of occupying the lady French polishers who were getting bored with having nothing to do. In time, first my father's Victorian oak desk, and then the equally Victorian dining room table could be seen in mid-air being hoisted to the French polishers' loft. There they had layers of brown Victorian varnish expertly removed and the grained wood surfaces made once more visible through transparent coatings of polyurethane. All I had to do was to pay periodic visits to the loft with an appropriate number of boxes of Black Magic.

French Polishers at Work

The big Firth of Clyde dry-dock, built at a cost of £5 million in 1960, next to the Kingston shipyard, was in answer to the Scottish grievance over the alleged lack of industrial investment in Scotland. Much of the money was found by the government of the day, with the equity subscribed by shipbuilders, engineers and the Scottish insurers, all of whose arms were twisted. It was opened with great pomp by the new company, chaired by General Sir Gordon Macmillan of the neighbouring Finlayston estate.

The dry-docking company only ever had one major dry-docking customer and that was the *Queen Elizabeth* in the winter of 1965–66. Even then a chunk had to be chopped out of one end of the dry-dock to accommodate the Queen's bow. I was involved in the survey of the Queen's hull bottom and that prompted one of my wittier colleagues to paint on the side of my white Morris Minor van, 'By Appointment to Queen Elizabeth, all Bottoms Examined and Other Inspections Speedily Carried Out'.

The anticipated demand for dry-docking of the large tankers after discharging at the Loch Long terminal did not materialise. The tanker

Visit by Tony Benn

managers found it more economical to clean tanks in the Atlantic, on
their way south, rather than in Port Glasgow, and to arrive at one of the
Mediterranean dry-docks with clean tanks. In the end the Firth of Clyde
Dry-dock Company wound up and the dry-dock was bought by Scotts
and Lithgow's at the knock-down price of little more than one million
pounds, to be used not only for repairs but for parking their completed
ships. Even when on one occasion Lithgow's needed to dry-dock their
own ship, a 250,000 ton tanker built in halves and joined afloat, she had
to be taken to Lisbon because their own dry-dock was not big enough.

Lithgow's shipyards and the Port Glasgow community, which largely
depended on them, survived the ups and downs of the shipping market
by sticking to the building of shelter deck cargo ships and of reasonably
sized, relatively uncomplicated bulk carriers and tankers. The crunch
came with the 1960s' Labour Government and the grand plans of Tony
Benn, Harold Wilson's Minister of Technology. Desperate attempts
were made to force Scotts and Lithgows to join the ill-starred and fated
Upper Clyde Shipbuilders. Inflation was spiralling out of control with
devastating consequences for the fixed price contracts that shipowners
demanded. Benn came to Port Glasgow in 1969 to tempt the now united

Erection of Goliath crane

Scott-Lithgow board to go in for building supertankers with a grant for constructing a super-crane, which was accepted. The burst in demand for supertankers, created by the 1967 Arab/Israeli war and the bypassing of the Suez Canal, however turned out to be quite temporary.

Lithgow's four 250,000 ton tankers were built in halves and successfully joined afloat. The work of developing the technique of joining the two parts of tankers afloat was interesting, and exciting particularly as the work had to be carried out in a tidal basin with a river current constantly flowing. It is to the credit of those concerned that four such operations were carried out without a mishap. The knowledge and methods so developed were used to join the deck of a semi-submersible to the legs and superstructure afloat off Greenock in 1983.

By the time the third and fourth supertankers were being completed, shipbuilding had been nationalised, demand had dwindled and the contracts were renegotiated at a loss by British Shipbuilders. This started the decline of Scott-Lithgow as a shipbuilding group. Hitherto the business had always been seen as sound. What completed the process was

Nordic Clansman joining up

when Scott-Lithgow were relegated to the Offshore Division of British Shipbuilders and were to build an oil rig and a semi-submersible and no more ships. At this time Scott's defence-related building programme was being terribly disrupted. Ministry of Defence specified and approved materials for four export submarines were found to be defective and this required comprehensive and lengthy refits, but the authorities had hushed this up. By 1983 a shipyard workforce to the tune of 2,500 was made redundant, leaving 2,000 until 1987. This precipitated a crisis for the Port Glasgow and Greenock communities. While the younger craftsmen could in time be retrained as computer technicians and programmers, some of the older ones had to swallow their pride in their crafts and eke out a living in relatively menial jobs.

World Score before join up

I was exiled from the Clyde to the south coast of England in 1976. By that time I was known in Port Glasgow and Greenock as Methuselah Weyndling because few people could remember the time when I wasn't there. The men of Lithgow's were so pleased to see me go that they presented me with a farewell flower picture for my wife by John Matheson, a friend and much-admired artist.

2
BOATYARDS

Bute Slip

Ardmaleish on the island of Bute seems to have been favoured by boat-builders for some time now. Beside the Bute Slip dockyard of Alfred Mylne senior, there was, before the Second World War, an adjoining boatyard run by Tom, Jack and Charlie Fife. At the Bute Slip yard yachts were being built of elegant lines and select timbers, mostly, if not always, to Alfred Mylne's design. Fifes built simple, traditional fishing boats, pitch pine planked and oak framed.

The interwar years were perhaps the golden era of the Mylne designs, when such distinguished craft as the 12-m 8-ton ketch *Jenetta* came out of the Bute yard. She was of novel construction as much as her having composite framing, her alternate frames being of steel and of steamed American elm, her keel too long to be of one piece being scarfed and jointed with a teak key and her mast being of hollowed Pacific spruce.

During that period the yard also built six Scottish Island Class, 5-ton sloop-rigged yachts to Alfred Mylne's design. That class was a very successful and popular compromise between the demands of racing and inshore cruising. The Dublin Bay Class 24-ft One Design, similar in concept to the Scottish Islands, but 8 ft longer overall, somewhat sleeker and with 25 per cent more sail area, was Alfred Mylne's swan song. Seven of them were built at Ardmaleish in the years just after the Second World War. Having these boats turned out in fairly quick succession brought the Ardmaleish yard back to working life after being a midget submarine base during the war.

It so happened that the owner/skipper of the Scottish Island *Gigha*, in which my friend and I used to crew, promoted himself in the early 1950s to a new Dublin Bay, *Periwinkle*. He sold *Gigha* to my co-crew member friend with whom I was to share running her and her running expenses. In the following summer, both boats took part in an overnight race out of Granton in the Firth of Forth, round Bass Rock and back. In the evening,

We were off Bass Rock by six o'clock

halfway down the Firth, the two boats came to a standstill, becalmed, with *Periwinkle* just about one boat's length ahead of *Gigha*. They anchored off the Fife shore, notorious for very light airs in the summer. About midnight we were still enjoying the warm summer night in *Gigha*'s cockpit when a light westerly air started gently to tickle our faces. There was nobody to be seen on board the *Periwinkle* but there was a sound of clinking glasses and of mild revelry emanating from under her coach roof. As the light air became a light breeze, we very quietly started to hoist our anchor, hand over hand because using the windlass might have annoyed the midnight party aboard the *Periwinkle*. All our sails went up and within minutes we were leaving the revellers' ship astern. *Periwinkle* never caught up with us during the rest of the night nor before the finishing line off Granton the following morning. And so our one-time skipper was overtaken by his once own crew. The bars of Scottish yacht clubs were for months after resounding to the story of the old Scottish Island beating the new Dublin Bay round Bass Rock.

Alfred senior died not very long after the war and the yard and design office passed into the hands of his nephew Alfred Mylne junior, who ran them both successfully for some twenty years. Alfred junior was, like his uncle, a gentleman boat designer and builder, and the day-to-day running of the boatyard was left to the yard manager, Bobbie Malcolm. During the 1960s the yard built a number of significant yachts, such as the 50-ton ketch *Glenafton*, the similar but slightly bigger *Naraina* and the steel framed, twin screw motor cruisers *Watonia III* and *Judi of Bute*.

In time it became clear that the boatyard could not survive on the building and fitting out of wooden yacht hulls. With the rapid onset of fibreglass material, a yard not equipped for producing fibreglass or steel hulls would have to accept the necessity of fitting out hulls manufactured elsewhere. With that in mind, in 1969 Alfred junior engaged Andrew Cumming, ex-manager of Maclean's boatyard in Renfrew, to take over as yard manager from Bobbie Malcolm.

First came *Lady Mavor*, a steel passenger motor vessel for the MoD. Next came *Albarka*, a 55-ft hospital ship for Lake Chad fitted into a fibreglass hull. *Albarka* was taken by sea to Lagos in Nigeria. From there it was intended to float her up the Niger river. However she was held up by the Nigerian Customs, who at first demanded a 'ransom' greater than the cost of the boat. By the time the vessel was released the water level of the Niger had become too low for the operation and it was decided to transport *Albarka* across Central Africa by a single track railway line. Andy accompanied his creation for most of the journey in the course of which it was sometimes necessary to dig under the rail to clear the boat under a bridge and sometimes to re-lay the track to get her round an obstacle. He got the ship to Lake Chad and there had to engineer her launching into the lake. Having searched for a suitable material for greasing the launch-ways he resorted in the end to local banana skins.

Orders for steel trawlers started coming in, six in total, soon after Andrew Cumming took over yard management. They were no longer designed by Mylne but by various steel fishing boat designers, such as Stuart MacAllister of Campbeltown. Similarly the building of steel hulls was entrusted to subcontractors such as George Brown's shipyard in Greenock.

The first of the trawlers to be built was the 70-ft transom stern *Trident*. She was subsequently lost with all hands in the Pentland Firth in 1972. The Formal Investigation held in Aberdeen Sheriff Court, in which I was involved, could not establish a definite cause of the *Trident*'s loss beyond surmising that she was probably overwhelmed by severe weather and sea conditions. I harbour a thought that small vessels with a fine bow, open fo'c'sle and transom stern are vulnerable to running themselves under in a following gale force wind and sea, due to having too much buoyancy aft. Alfred Mylne seems to have felt himself, as builder of the *Trident*, liable for her loss and put the Bute Slip dock into voluntary liquidation.

The yard was in 1974 taken over by brothers Stan and Maxwell Ferguson and has been successfully run by them and their sons to this day. While long established West Coast boatyards such as Macleans of Renfrew, Dickies of Tarbert and Adams of Gourock had to close, Fergusons' yard well survived the revolution in boat building caused by keen competition from numerous fibreglass hull moulders and the diminishing demand for wood boat-building crafts. Ardmaleish Boatyard has been annually overhauling up to fifty fishing boats and Calmac ferries, and could cope with up to four vessels at any one time. They've kept the flag of West Coast boat-building flying high to this day!

Fife's of Fairlie

The Fife yard at Fairlie has had a glorious history, started by a William Fyfe with his first real yacht *Lamlash* in 1812 and in 1814 with the *Industry*, the first steamer with a paddle box, and which had a working life of fifty-five years. Its golden era came towards the end of the nineteenth century when William Fife senior and junior were both designers and yard managers. Their designs, built at Fairlie, were made distinct by their fiddle bows. A dragon head was carved on the bow, continuing as a thin line to the stern where it ended in a wheat sheaf, the whole carving was gilded. The bow carvings created a boom for ship carvers.

The dragon carvings may have had a connection with Fairlie's Viking past and the defeat of the Vikings at the Battle of Largs in the thirteenth century. On the other hand it might have been the phenomenal racing success of the three *Dragon* yachts designed and built by Fife's that prompted William to use the dragon logo as his trademark. Just before the First World War, Sir Thomas Lipton turned to William Fife junior for his Americas Cup challengers, such as the *Shamrock*.

Yacht building continued between the wars with William Fife junior designing and the yard management passed to his nephew Balderston Fife whose not very competitive costing tended to lose some possible orders. The emergence of new smaller yacht racing classes was a reflection of the post-war state of the economy. William was approached and designed fifteen boats of the Conway Class suitable for racing and day cruising, of optional rig but restricted to 20 foot length. They were all built by A.M. Dickie of Bangor, North Wales, who had an earlier association with the Fife yard. Archibald Dickie, founder of Dickie's of Tarbert yard, had been an employee of Fife. His son Peter Dickie served his apprenticeship with Fife at Fairlie and then set up Dickie's of Bangor. Shortly before the last war Fife's built their largest yacht *Mariella*, a 78-ft Bermudian yawl constructed of steel frames and teak planking. She was designed by Alfred Mylne who wrote to Balderston Fife asking for the cost of £11,275 to be reduced. *Mariella* is still to the fore. She took part in the Sidney to Hobart race in 1990, and in 1994 and 1995 won the Antigua Classic Yacht Regatta.

The yard was closed to yacht building for the duration of the Second World War and given over to building for war purposes. A Mr Calder was appointed by the Admiralty to take charge. He was an efficient manager but I found him barely visible behind a cigarette smoke screen. After the war the yard was bought by a former customer who put in Archibald (Baldie) Macmillan, a foreman rigger, as manager. Baldie was well into the yard management and he had Jeannie well into running the yard office when I started calling at regular intervals in the late 1950s.

The ring-netter *Ocean Maid* was being built at Fairlie for John Macmillan of Carradale in the 1960s. The launch was to be preceded by a little lunch reception at the Fairlieburn Hotel at Fairlie. For some reason I was invited to sit at the top table with Mr and Mrs Archibald Macmillan, Mr and Mrs John Macmillan and an inspector from the Scottish Herring Board. Conversation at the top table progressed to a point at which the boat-builder Macmillans and the boat-owner Macmillans became disinclined to communicate directly. This made the Herring Board man and myself into conveyors of messages diagonally across the lunch table. In fact we became found ourselves emulating Dr Kissinger, who had to mediate between opposing Middle Eastern parties by to-ing and fro-ing between them while they sat in separate rooms.

The diplomatic situation was not improved by the events at the launch ceremony. All was as usual at those occasions: men in their Sunday suits, ladies in their Sunday hats and the ship's godmother with a huge bouquet of flowers in one hand and a bottle of 'bubbly' in the other, all expectant on the platform. The signal was given to knock out the wedges that held the vessel on the ways, the wedges were knocked out, the 'bubbly' was dripping from the bows, the *Ocean Maid* moved down the ways a few inches and then stopped. The ladies and gentlemen, the godmother with the bouquet of flowers still in the launching position, all froze for a while on the platform. Then, nudged by their wives, the Sunday-suited men slowly stepped down and started to encourage the obstinate boat to move down the way.

The assisted downward movement continued inch by inch and in due course the gentlemen were obliged to take off their socks and shoes to coax the hull into the water. When the launch party began to roll up their trousers above their knees, a Carradale skipper Archie Paterson and myself formed an emergency committee, which quickly decided to phone the skipper of a 70-ft, 200-hp fishing vessel at Maidens in Ayrshire. She came and saved the day by towing the *Ocean Maid* till she came afloat.

Floating the new ship did not resolve the political impasse. The next item on the day's agenda was a trial trip combined with a maiden voyage. From this, Baldie chose to abstain for diplomatic reasons and to send a lesser mortal in his place. He thought that his principal function as host would have been to preside over the bar on board and this function he bequeathed to me, presumably considered as a neutral body. Looked at in that way, it could have been taken as an honour that had to be graciously accepted. A thought, only briefly, crossed my mind that the powers that be in London might not have visualised bar tending on the trial trip of a fishing boat as one of a Board of Trade surveyor's duties.

Dickie's of Tarbert

The boatyard of Dickie's of Tarbert goes back to 1885, when Archie Dickie went there from Fife's of Fairlie and started boat-building on his own account.

View of Tarbert

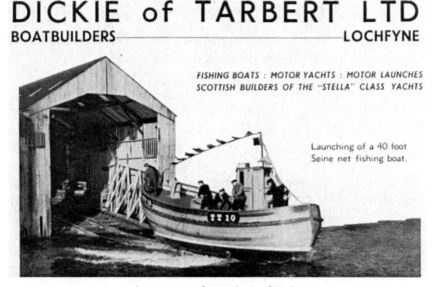

DICKIE of TARBERT LTD
BOATBUILDERS ———————————— **LOCHFYNE**

FISHING BOATS : MOTOR YACHTS : MOTOR LAUNCHES
SCOTTISH BUILDERS OF THE "STELLA" CLASS YACHTS

Launching of a 40 foot
Seine net fishing boat.

TT 10

Advertisement for Dickie's of Tarbert

After the First World War Archie's son Peter managed the yard for a time, but in 1923 he went to Bangor in North Wales to start a 'Dickie's' yard there. Another son Tom took over the yard management. Bob Dickie looked after the engineering work, Jim Dickie the blacksmith's work and father Archie stayed on as the slip foreman. By 1928 when Archie died, the yard had been extended to build all kinds of sailing and motor boats up to 100 ft in length. It employed a foreman boat-builder in charge of ten boat-builders, four apprentice boat-builders, three blacksmiths, two slip labourers, two painters and one sawyer, not to speak of a timekeeper and an office girl.

In 1936 the yard suffered a Calor gas explosion on the yacht *Jumma*. The whole hull of the boat above the waterline and all its contents were blown high into the air, but the deckhand was picked up from the water unharmed. His escape was due to the fact that he was in the centre of the explosion and everything was blown away around him. In 1937 Dickies designed and built *Tunnag* a 44-ft auxiliary ketch and *Crunneag* a 64-ft one for Mr Morton of Kilmarnock carpets. These were varnished teak, gentleman's motor-yachts, the like of which we shall never see again. One of the last boats to come out of Dickie's yard before the outbreak of war in 1939 was the 60-ft motorboat *Darthula* for Sandy Black, for cruises on Loch Etive, of which more in another chapter.

Bill Waight

During the Second World War the yard produced six Fairmile 112-ft motor launches, eight Fairmile 115-ft motor torpedo boats and a number of motor fishing vessels, all to Admiralty orders. After the war, in 1946, Dickies built a few fishing boats for local fishermen and in the following year they gave up boat-building.

I started visiting the yard regularly in the late 1950s. It had earlier been resuscitated by Raymond Aitchison, a politically active gentleman, who, with the blessing of the then Secretary of State Michael Noble, assembled a conclave of professional, mostly Edinburgh, men to be his co-directors at Dickie's. The company was called Highland Engineering Ltd. Raymond Aitchison's brother-in-law, Patrick Banks, was appointed yard manager. Patrick was a practical man, which perhaps made up for his not having the benefit of a boat-building background.

The brains behind Dickie's boat-building and boat designing at the time was Bill Waight, a native of the Isle of Wight. He was a brother-in-law of Uffa Fox, with whom he worked and to some of whose designs he significantly contributed. Bill exiled himself to Tarbert after the demise of the jointly owned Medina yard in the late 1950s. It didn't take long for this Sassenach, and his wife Vera, to be amongst the most popular figures in the village. Bill's sense of fun, his gift for simplifying complex problems, his happy outlook on life and reluctance to take himself seriously matched the Highland philosophy. He designed a number of yachts and fishing boats built in Tarbert at the time. Two or three of

Kyles of Bute ferry

the successful 28-ft clinker hull ferry boats for short sea crossings built in Crinan boatyard bore a very close resemblance to Bill's design. The fact that a boat-builder who worked in Dickie's yard, and his daughter who ran the yard office, moved to Crinan when Dickie's stopped boat-building, may be a sheer coincidence.

My calls on Dickie's Yard were particularly frequent in the early 1960s when the ill-fated Kyles of Bute ferry was being built there for the Marquess of Bute and, by his lordship's request, as much as possible with timber from his own estate. 'Streamlining' of management resulted in both Patrick and Bill having gone by the time the ferry was being completed.

Two men come to mind from the ferry building era at Dickie's. One was Ian Nicholson, a partner of Alfred Mylne, who designed the ferry. He would occasionally give me a lift to Tarbert in his natty sports car. To say the journeys were exciting would be an understatement. My fingers used to turn blue gripping whatever I could while Ian sped up the narrow, old Rest and Be Thankful road. The very same Ian was a delightfully unhurried person in his sailing boat *St Elisabeth*, which he built himself and in which he crossed the Atlantic. Once, when his mother and I crewed for him, he left the helm to us for the whole day while he and his wife were busy below with their new infant. The other was James Macfarlane, Dickie's foreman carpenter, firemaster of Tarbert, and a thorough gentleman. One Monday I drew his attention to a young boat-builder driving a steel fastening into the wooden structure without first dipping it in white lead as was the usual procedure at that time. 'You will

Ian Nicholson & Alfred Mylne

have to forgive him this time,' James responded, 'He was late to bed last night and hasn't yet come round.' The only aggressive feature of James was his whistle which he carried round his neck and with which he used to call the men to and off work. He was generally known as 'Blarney'.

Sometime in 1967 the yard was bought by an English north-east coast man by the name of Peter Kaye. He also bought Dickie's ship chandlers and one or two Tarbert hotels. Peter harboured the conviction that what Tarbert needed was to be brought into the modern times with the blessings of fast transport. Hovercraft were the flavour of the year and Peter decided to adopt hovercraft for an express service between Tarbert and Gourock, via Dunoon and Rothesay. The Dickies' boat-building slips were demolished to be replaced by a concrete hovercraft landing and parking ramp, and a hovercraft revealed itself along with three glamorous hover-hostesses.

Hovercraft in the Kyles of Bute

Peter Kaye concluded from his market research that the average number of passengers daily arriving at Tarbert on the *Lochfyne* from Gourock, Dunoon and Rothesay was thirty-six, and by a fortunate coincidence that was exactly the number of passenger seats on the hovercraft. Since he sought my opinion I ventured to guess that passengers arriving on the *Lochfyne* were not of the kind who would be inclined to double the cost of their passage so as to reduce the two-hour sea journey to one hour. Some were in transit and arrived at East Loch Tarbert pier in nice time to do leisurely the one-mile crossing to the *Lochiel* at West Loch Tarbert pier to take them to Gigha, Islay or Jura. Some were Tarbert housewives, who having spent one or two days shopping in Glasgow, were in no great hurry to get back home. Some were commercial travellers, who, if they came by *Lochfyne*, were spending a night in a Tarbert hotel, and if they were aiming at returning within a day, came by car.

The hovercraft service opened with much pomp and circumstance but passengers did not flock to it to justify its existence. Had some of the male passengers a chance to set eyes on the bonny hover-hostesses they would surely have been tempted to travel. Peter did not abandon the West Coast after the demise of the hovercraft venture and he bought the island of Little Cumbrae in the Firth of Clyde for his summer residence. It would have been the idyllic island retreat were it not for lack of telephone communication. In order to persuade the Post Office, who were then also responsible for telephones, to install a line he arranged for telegrams to be sent to him daily, and these had to be delivered daily by a courier in a specially hired boat. After a few weeks of daily deliveries the Postmaster decreed that the telegrams be delivered weekly. At that stage the Laird of Little Cumbrae decided to lay down his own telephone cable. At the end of the summer a supply of submarine cable was assembled on the island for use the following spring. However with the coming of spring it transpired that Little Cumbrae field mice had had many field days feasting on the submarine cable insulation.

Dickie's yard survived as over-winter parking for boats until 1985. For a time it was run for that purpose by Cochran Duncan of Ayr whom I remember as a very young man from our days in the Glasgow University Air Squadron in the last war. In 1985 the site was sold to the Barr Construction Company of Ayr.

Crinan Boatyard

Crinan Boatyard was founded by Blair Wilson in 1961. Shortly after leaving the Navy, he came into possession of an aunt's croft at Crinan. A Board of Trade loan helped him to start a boatyard there, in a sheltered harbour and an advantageous position: there was no commercial boat repairing facility on the Atlantic coast of Scotland between Campbeltown and Mallaig.

One of the earlier boat-building achievements of the Crinan yard was a series of 28-ft clinker-built wood motor launches to a design of Bill

28 ft ferry boat built at Crinan

Waight's, of which there is more earlier in this chapter when recalling Dickie's yard in Tarbert. At least two of them were ordered by Argyll County Council for passenger ferry service to Gigha and Lismore. There followed a number of 17-ft motor launches of similar design. Otherwise the yard was busy re-engining fishing boats, inevitably with ever more powerful Kelvin engines, supplied directly by Bergius Works in Glasgow.

The year 1966 was commercially successful enough for the Crinan Yard for it to be able to start repaying the Board of Trade loan at £83 per month, to install a new slipping winch and to create an engine shop. A major boatbuilding success came in 1967 when the *Island Lass*, a 45-ft motor passenger launch was delivered to Mrs Henrietta Spencer in Oban to her satisfaction. This achievement was however not without problems for the boat-builder. The boat suffered some damage when, after launching, she was carried away from her mooring by a storm and landed ashore. Financially, the *Island Lass* proved to be a loss. I was directed by the Board of Trade headquarters to ask for safety provisions that were not in the original specification and the cost of these could not be passed to the customer because of the fixed price contract

In 1967 Dickie's boatyard in Tarbert was closed. Blair Wilson was approached about taking over that yard and running it in conjunction with the Crinan one. The proposal was stalled by the owning partnership, called Highland Engineering Ltd, asking £25,000 for the yard, valued at £8,000 to £10,000. Another contemplated possibility was the formation of a consortium of the Crinan, Dickie's and MacGruer's boatyards. Negotiations on those lines went on throughout the year without reaching a conclusion. Towards the end of the year Crinan Boatyard began to suffer from credit squeeze and reduction in the availability of overdraft and a MacGruer's offer to buy the yard for £7,000 came under consideration. In the end MacGruer's withdrew their interest as they were getting engaged in a new Admiralty contract.

Early in 1968 the yard was sold to Mr & Mrs Humphrey Massey for about £8,000. In the severe storm of that winter two boats, Mrs Spencer's newly built *Island Lass* and the *Islander*, a converted US Navy personnel carrier, were washed away from the Crinan Boatyard slip. The insurers refused to pay for the damage because they considered it an 'Act of God'.

There was not much new building in Massey's times and my visits to the yard were mainly in connection with re-surveys of county passenger boats and sometimes trying to persuade the owner of a small flotilla of cattle carrying craft to meet the basic safety standard. The owner in question

Donald Ross' *Cyclops*

was Donald Ross, an intrepid and daring sailor, a buoyant character who would have been in his element in the buccaneering days, or as a Francis Drake-like pirate-hero. His craft ranged from *Look and See*, an ex-lifeboat of the *Mauretania*, to *Cyclops*, an ex-naval pinnace. These boats, packed with cattle and with the minimum of crew, made trips to the grazing islands, which were often eventful, to put it mildly, and tales of their adventures circulated far and wide.

Donald's boats used to have 'unofficial repairs' carried out at Crinan Boatyard and these would bring them up to Donald Ross' rather than the Board of Trade's standard of safety. Either my reprobation of Donald's 'modus vivendi' was becoming a bit more effective, or his conscience had started to prick him at last, because one weekend, while at my mother's house in Edinburgh, I received a phonecall and an invitation from him. In his 'hideaway' above his fashionable *Aperitif* restaurant in Edinburgh's Frederick Street he tried, over a glass of vintage port, to arrive with me at a compromise between the Board of Trade's and Donald Ross' safety rules for boats carrying cattle and men to wee uninhabited islands.

Although it was employing skilled boat-builders, such as the 'heid yin' Neil Cameron, Ian Sutherland and Roni Gilbert, the yard's bread-and-butter job was refitting fishing boats and yachts. Slipping them could be quite fun as it was recognized that any bottles found on board in

Roni Gilbert

the course of slipping were to be 'taken prisoner' to avoid them getting splintered in the process.

It was in Massey's time that the photograph of the motor launch *Happy Days* on the slip of Crinan Boatyard was taken. The 38-ft boat, of slender, somewhat Kelvin launch-like hull, was built in 1926 by Noble of Irvine. She had a slightly top-heavy cabin top and twin Perkins engines when she turned up as one of Ian MacKechnie's ferries on the Tayinloan to Gigha crossing. It was not long before she was replaced by the new purpose-built ferry and found her way into the possession of the landlord of a Campbeltown hotel. He entrusted the boat to a local joiner with somewhat scanty experience of boat work, because she was suffering from wood worm and generally needed repairing. Once out of the joiner's care *Happy Days* was advertised for sale.

My wife's cousins who came to live in the Kyles of Bute were looking for a motorboat of that size and I showed them *Happy Days* with a warning of not touching her with a barge pole. Needless to say they fell in love with her. I was in the hotel landlord's wee office when the cousin in question phoned and offered to buy the boat. I had to tell him that the figure the landlord was looking for was £600, although I thought it was too much and could not say so. When the cousin said that he appreciated the amount of repair work the present owner had done on the boat and offered £1,000,

Aerial view of Crinan Boatyard

I nearly choked. In the circumstances all I could do was pass on the offer, which was promptly accepted and the boat effectively sold. It was the only time I could remember that that nearly teetotal landlord produced a large dram on the house.

That night, my wife and I went late to bed and were, for once, able to listen to the midnight Scottish radio news. One of the early items was on the Campbeltown lifeboat having been called out to a local motorboat called *Happy Days*, which was stranded on a rock off Davaar Island. I could hardly believe my ears and early next morning phoned the hotel landlord. He replied indignantly to my query: 'You talk as if it was the Wreck of the *Hesperus*!' The same joiner did his standard style of repairs, the cousins paid the originally promised amount and the boat spent a lot of her remaining days in Crinan Boatyard.

The ownership of the yard passed from the Masseys to the Stewarts (Mr Stewart had been a naval diver), during whose time the yard was set on fire, being rebuilt in steel. Proprietors changed again in 1995 and eventually the yard went into receivership. John Dunlop, an engineer

Launch *Happy Days*

from Skipness, took over in 1999 and persuaded the creditors to form a company. He built a new shed with enough headroom for boat-building under cover. At the time of writing the boatyard appears to be doing well under John's management, mainly on repairing wooden and steel fishing boats, fish farm vessels and yachts, and storing up to sixty boats. He plans to start boat-building, perhaps even wood hulls.

McGruer's of Clynder

Since my earliest days on the Clyde I learnt to think of McGruer as being in the Rolls Royce class of Scottish boat-builders, rivalled perhaps only by Robertson of Sandbank, Fife of Fairlie and Alfred Mylne's Bute Slip dock in their heydays.

The McGruers, having moved from Rutherglen via Glasgow Green and Sandbank to Tighnabruaich, made their final move from Tighnabruaich to Clynder on the Rosneath Peninsula, carrying all their belongings in a Clyde puffer and set up a boat-building yard there in 1910. They had become significant already in the First World War by producing the hollow spar, which found a multiplicity of applications from the boom of the Royal Yacht *Britannia* to struts of fighter planes and bombers.

James (left) and Willie McGruer at their drawing board

In the 1920s Ewing McGruer junior, one of seven sons of Ewing senior, designed the beautiful and fast 24-ft Bermudian rigged sloop Gareloch One Design to be built of pitch pine planking, elm timbers and with solid spruce spars. Sixteen of them were built and named after Greek gods and goddesses, all sixteen of them are racing in the Gareloch to this day. Five of Alfred Mylne's Scottish Islands One Design were built at McGruer in the early 1930s.

About the same time Ewing junior met in London Johan Anker, the Norwegian designer of the Dragon, and by 1936 McGruer started building Dragon One Design yachts, sloop-rigged and of 29-ft overall length, which became an Olympic class. McGruer built altogether forty-four Dragons in timber, the last one was the *Bintyra*, built in 1950 for Sir James Millar, a Lord Provost of Edinburgh and later a Lord Mayor of London. She was sailed out of Granton and I had the privilege of crewing in her at one time.

Dragon Number 25 was built by McGruer sometime in the 1930s and christened the *Moonbeam*. In the early 1960s she was donated to Keil

Ketch *Ceresio* designed by George McGruer launching from Clynder Yard

School in Dumbarton and renamed *Lucy,* the name *Moonbeam* having been transferred to a newer Dragon. I was one of the two sailing instructors on *Lucy* for the Keil School boys. When the Keil School decided to dispose of her, my family bought her for the asking price of £200, the younger members of the family contributing £5 each of their saved up pocket money. And so *Lucy* became a member of the author's family. A wee connection with McGruer was retained: while measuring yachts at McGruer, I was always welcome to look over the building drawings of my 'ship' which was useful when maintenance repairs or renewals were to be done. *Lucy* ended her sailing days at the Scottish Maritime Museum at Irvine.

In 1930, at the age of twenty-four, James McGruer went to America to work with Herreshoff and gain design experience with particular regard to rating rules. At that time the J class yacht *Enterprise* was under construction there and James worked on her spars and rigging. Later he was asked to report for some Glasgow newspapers on the America's Cup challenge races between the *Enterprise* and *Shamrock V.*

Of the bigger yachts that came out of the McGruer stable before the

Gareloch One design *Thalia*, *Teal*, *Zephyrus* and *Catriona*, designed by Ewing McGruer, racing in the Gareloch

Second World War, the most outstanding was perhaps the *Northward*, a 50-ft long sailing vessel, built to Alfred Mylne's design, of which Cecil Day Lewis, Poet Laureate, wrote a poem in 1930:

> Under a hillside by sunny Gareloch,
> Scaring the cormorant off his wave-perch, floated
> Forth on the springtime into my element
> I, the yacht NORTHWARD.
>
> Seven brothers built my body of oak and elm,
> Woke in the dumb wood a spirit of seafaring,
> Hoisted the spruce to command a new world . . .

The seven McGruer brothers were truly a working team. Ewing was the inventor and the intellectual front runner of the team, John the workforce man, Willie the business head, David the timber authority, Alec the service manager, Andrew the hollow spar expert and sister Jessie ran the company's office. The seventh brother James took over from Ewing as the inspired designer. He trained with G.L. Watson in Glasgow and back home, after the spell in America, designed Six-Metres with a very effective underwater hull form. There was, of course, no yacht building during the Second World War but McGruer turned out twenty five 72-ft Harbour Defence Motor Launches for the Admiralty.

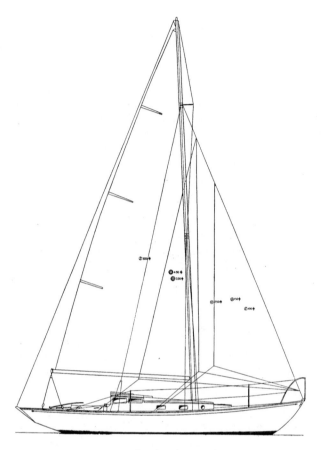

Bermudan ketch *Romela*

After the war James responded to the growing demand by designing and producing a number of Eight-Metre cruiser-racers, which were nearly 40 feet in overall length, including some 12 feet of bow and stern overhangs. They had laminated frames, teak planking below waterline and mahogany above. By the time I came to be a caller at McGruer in the late 1950s there was hardly anything smaller than an Eight-Metre cruiser-racer being built there. James' *Inismara* built in 1963, which I had the pleasure of measuring, outraced eight other Eight-Metres the day she was launched and won that year's Lloyd's Trophy.

The three decades I can remember, the 1950s, '60s and '70s, were perhaps the golden years of the McGruer saga under James as managing director from 1956 and his son George from 1976. In the 1970s they bought from the Admiralty the former American base at Rosneath, consisting of twelve parallel sheds, and moved there from Clynder. McGruer became the largest boatyard on the Clyde, building more Eight-Metre-cruiser-racers and some bigger craft. Ewing would appear from time to time, when he could tear himself away from advising the Scottish Industrial Development Trust in Edinburgh, and would take it upon himself to teach the younger McGruer generations sealore and safety afloat.

In 1986, with James hale and hearty at eighty, a home-born poet expounded:

> On the life of this man who hails from the Kyles,
> A life of design and nautical miles . . .

and went on:

> On oceans and lochs, on rivers and channels
> This dapper wee man in blazer and flannels
> Has been feted, respected, had his praises sung.
> He's not eighty years old – just eighty years young.

In the 1990s a number of McGruer's old wooden boats returned to the yard for restoration which helped to maintain traditional wood boat-building skills. In 1992 a newly designed 24-ft sloop *Amber* was built in wood and finished in bronze by yard trainees under the Skillbuild scheme. In 1994 a wooden boat enthusiast cousin Fraser Noble took over as managing director, with George McGruer as chairman. The yard celebrated its centenary by restoring the Clyde 17/19 *Wyvette* built in 1897.

At the time of writing the firm, under Fraser Noble, has turned into surveyors, brokers, project managers and archivists of McGruer designed and built vessels.

Port Bannatyne

The Port Bannatyne boatyard, which was started by Archie Malcolm in 1905, was taken over by Peter MacIntyre in 1934 and assumed his name. Donald MacIntyre succeeded to the yard sometime after the war. He was a county councillor, a garage owner, a farmer, a Lloyds agent, the commodore of the local yacht club and presided over a few professional and charitable societies besides. The boatyard, which needed more than his spare time, was successfully managed by Hamish Weir with Neillie Macqueen as his foreman.

A distinctive feature of the boatyard from 1939 until about 1970 was the elegant silhouette of *Lady Guildford*, a sailing yacht built in the early nineteenth century to bring the bride of the then Marquess of Bute to the island. From the 1970s she was replaced, sometimes in the yard but mostly in Rothesay harbour, by the 80-ft long brigantine (square rig on the main mast and fore-and-aft on the mizzen) *Joven Teresa*, which with her tall masts and a striking figurehead made a captivating sight.

Joven Teresa was a local trader at Ibiza and was bought by Walter Bergius, the managing director of Teacher's whisky, to be converted to a yacht. She spent several years with Peter MacIntyre's to be abandoned in the end. Walter, although deaf from birth, managed to master the art of communication and used to get impatient with me as I found it difficult to understand him at first when discussing the work on his yacht to be.

Donald MacIntyre's wife Marjorie – who looked like balm for sore eyes, and still does! – used to run Rothesay Harbour Marina bar and restaurant. The bar shelves were lined with bottles of Teacher's of all shapes and sizes. I once asked Donald if his customer was paying him in kind. He said, 'No, he's just being kind to me.'

Sometime in the early 1970s I was surveying a small passenger vessel under construction at Peter MacIntyre's yard. Ordered by the naval establishment at Greenock, it was intended for conveying daily the civilian personnel from Gourock to the naval installation on Loch Long. The building of the boat was proceeding smoothly, with frequent exchanges between Hamish Weir and myself to ensure compliance with the current statutory rules for passenger vessels. When it came to fire protection, and the cost of it, the naval paymasters decided that the boat was to be finished to naval rather than merchant navy rules, as they did not require so much structural fire protection. This threw into disarray the plans laid down between Hamish and myself, but even more troublesome was the cry of protest from a number of local passenger boat operators whose boats were having to compete against a boat that didn't have to comply with all the costly passenger boat rules. They met me and asked me to take the matter up with the Naval Office Commanding in the Navy Building in which my office was located. That was how I became *persona non grata* with my 'landlord'!

Donald, a vital personality of the island, known as 'MacIntyre of Bute', was bravely standing up to illness and was as hospitable and as charming as ever when I last saw him in the spring of 2004. Peter MacIntyre's is alas no longer a working boatyard.

Campbeltown Shipyard

Campbeltown Shipyard, small but hardly a boatyard, was dormant for some forty years from the 1920s. It was first resuscitated in the late 1960s by Thames Launch Works with John Alban as managing director and John Carmichael, a local engineer, as yard manager.

The English boat-builders' interest in the enterprise did not last very long but Sir William Lithgow came to the rescue, a valiant act of faith on his part and no mean contribution to Campbeltown's search for employment. The management of the yard was given to Leslie Howarth. Under his, and earlier under John Carmichael's direction, a number of steel fishing vessels were built, initially small ones for the Kintyre fishing fleet but then quite big ones, mostly for the East Coast based Scottish fleet.

My special concern was the building for Argyll County Council of *Belnahua* – named after one of the Slate Islands – the new car ferry for the Cuan Sound, powerful enough to operate at all states of tide. The county council made sure that not only the builders but also the designer was of Argyll. He was A. Boyd of Sandbank, well known for designing the *Sceptre* the first post-war Americas Cup challenger. He completed plans for the usual kind of double-ended roll-on-roll-off vehicular ferry just as the county council decided, on grounds of economy, to reduce the

Cuan Sound ferry *Belnahua*

ship's length. It needed a yacht designer to solve the ensuing problem by installing the ramps at diagonally opposite corners!

The essentially standardised [in the Lithgow tradition] Campbeltown boats were around 80 feet over all and ordered by fishing skippers who were part-owners of these vessels. The staff and workforce had very high standards and, despite Campbeltown's remoteness from the main fishing ports of the Scottish East Coast, the leading skippers beat a path to the door of this yard where their very complex boats were designed by Leslie Howarth and Douglas MacNaught, built under cover and fitted out alongside.

The yard ceased production in the 1990s due to the decline of the fishing industry. John Carmichael still runs a busy engineering workshop in Campbeltown.

3

FISHING BOAT TALES

I came across the motor fishing vessel *May* in the command of Lachlan Clark of Port Ellen, Islay, in Tarbert harbour sometime in the autumn. 'Mister Clark' I said, 'You don't seem to have much in the way of life-saving equipment. No life jackets, no lifebuoys, no rockets . . '

'Captain Clark to you,' said Lachie. 'Do you mean to tell me I need all those things? Nobody tells me anything.'

'See you in a month's time, Captain,' were my parting words.

'How the time flies. It wouldn't be a month already?' was Lachie's greeting when I stepped on board five weeks later. 'You wouldn't like a nice bit of lobster?' I hadn't much choice but to give him one more month.

Before a month was up, a letter arrived with an Islay postmark. It read: 'Dear Mister Board of Trade. The vessel *May* will be available for inspection in the port of Bowmore on Christmas Day. I'll have all the things you asked for, except for the distress rockets. I have been in that many distresses, I used them all up.'

I promptly wrote back: 'Dear Captain Clark, I'd like fine to spend Christmas on board your ship in the port of Bowmore; but I'd also much like to see your new supply of distress rockets. Wouldn't New Year's Day do?'

The reply was postmarked Oban: 'Dear Mister Surveyor' it said. 'I have now all the things you asked for but it is no use your coming after the *May* to Oban because by the time you come, she will be gone. Yours faithfully, Captain Lachlan Clark.'

The good ship *May* finally came to grief off the coast of Islay sometime in August 1968. Captain Lachlan's previous fishing boat, by the name of *Ile Bhòidheach* (Beautiful Islay) was driven ashore at Ardnave, on the north-west shore of Islay, due to a slipping clutch. Both Lachie and his crew, 'Doicks' Macallister were rescued, but Lachie should have known better than to allow 'Islay' in his boat's name. Apparently nothing can be more unlucky. Earlier, before the war, while in a family croft at Kilchiaran,

At Tarbert Fish Quay

Lachie used to fish locally with his father, in an open skiff. When that boat was overcome, he swam ashore – with his father on his back.

One of my duties, while on the West Coast of Scotland, was inspecting fishing boats for safety equipment. It was not a job to be hurried. One would happen to be on the fish quay when the first of the fleet came alongside and one would, for lack of anything else to do, haul up a few fish-boxes. The skipper knew who you were and you knew who he was, but nothing was said.

'Fishing any good today?', one opened at last. 'Bloody awful.' came the inevitable reply. After a while one would venture 'Not a bad day.' He would say 'No.' and away we'd go hauling up in silence. Again nothing was said till all the boxes were on the quay and then, 'You may as well come on board for a cup of tea.' As we'd settled down round the saloon table, and something like tea had been poured out of a lemonade bottle, the skipper would casually let go, 'As you are here you might as well do the safety gear!'

Inspections were not always as light-hearted as this, and the ensuing situations not always as undramatic. Big Bob was a Carradale fisherman but I came upon his boat at Tarbert's fish quay. His second hand was doing his best, but there wasn't really much he could show me on board. Just as I got to the point of listing the missing equipment, the skipper himself emerged from the hostelry across the road. He shuffled towards me zig-zag fashion, a wee spirit glass in each hand. 'Mister Surveyor, will ye do me the honour of having a wee Drambuie with me?', he proposed in the middle of the fish quay. One of the local skippers materialised beside me like a deus ex machina and whispered loudly: 'Mister Surveyor, there is a wee refreshment already laid on for you at the Tarbert Hotel.' He propelled me in that direction, whispering less loudly, 'I thought I'd spare you the embarassment of having to cope with that stotious Carradale lot.' We had coffee and a sandwich and a dram, and before leaving my rescuer declared, 'I would not offend you Sir, by offering to pay. It might smack of bribery and corruption!'

While on that subject, I was only once offered a bribe. It was at the time when a new rule came into force obliging every fishing boat of twenty-five or more registered tons to carry a certificated skipper; or at least, one with a second hand's special certificate. A well-known Carradale skipper felt that he was past swotting for the exams and that it might be more expedient to persuade the surveyor to reduce his ship's registered tonnage. With that in mind, he slipped a fiver into my pocket. It would have been a bit heavy-handed in the ethereal atmosphere of Carradale to delve into the ethical and philosophical aspects of bribery, and into the structural impracticability of reducing ship's tonnage. I picked up the note with two fingers, 'You hold it for a while skipper. I have got holes in my pockets. What about a wee dram on the strength of it later today?'

A follow-up to this little incident produced a weekend gathering in one of the four bars of Campbeltown's Argyll Arms Hotel. I twisted the arms of skippers of the bigger Campbeltown, Carradale and Tarbert boats to meet me. I wanted to hear why they were reluctant to have a go at a relatively non-academic exam. The reason most of them gave me was the need to attend for a few days at the Glasgow Nautical College and so waste precious fishing time. In response to that I persuaded Captain MacCallum to take on a weekend class for the fishing boat skippers and second hands. He had recently retired to the quiet Kintyre township of Clachan from having been imparting his nautical knowledge in the South Pacific. The attendance at the class was at first most impressive, but it fell with succeeding weekends. Perhaps one could excuse the men

Carradale fishing fleet

who had to be up at five on most days for being averse to getting up on weekend mornings.

There used to be an efficient bush telegraph system operating between the fishing communities in Scotland. It would go into action the moment I left Inveraray heading southwards through Knapdale and down the Kintyre peninsula. It would take me nearly two hours to drive from Inveraray to Campbeltown but the message that 'Board of Trade' was on his way would get there in half that time. A frequent change of colour and style of one's car was, in the circumstances, to be recommended. I was once Carradale bound and bent on seeing Donnelly Macmillan, skipper of the fishing boat *Marie*. The Carradale postmistress, the fountainhead of all local knowledge, was my first port of call in search of Donnelly's whereabouts. 'Donnelly, Donnelly,' she readily offered, 'It's not five minutes since he left here. He'll either have gone to his mother's up Woodside way, or else back home to Torrisdale. Get you in your car and try Torrisdale first, two miles down the road.' Away I went and was in Torrisdale in no more than five minutes. Now, there was no such thing as a telephone in Donnelly's house in those days, and needless to say there were no mobile telephones. And there was Donnelly outside his house smiling a welcome. 'Wife has a kettle on for a cup of tea. We have been expecting you.'

Carradale

The bush telegraph functioned quite well in the days when surveyors did not have cars in which to chase from harbour to harbour. In the late 1940s and the early 1950s, I used to visit the fishing fleet at St Monance in Fife, from time to time, by train from Edinburgh. There were no inflatable life-rafts in those days, but fishing boats over a certain size were obliged to carry miniature lifeboats ready for launching in emergency. Such fishing vessels as complied with this rule and carried wee lifeboats would put them to good use by stowing in them potatoes and fresh vegetables. The station in St Monance was a good twenty minutes walk away from the pier. The moment I stepped off the train the bush telegraph went into action. By the time I walked to the pier, not only were the available lifeboats thoroughly emptied of tatties, but they had also been transferred to the first few boats I was liable to encounter. When these had been inspected, I would be invited to step below 'for a cup of tea'. I had a weird suspicion that the wee lifeboats were then being passed from the boats I had already seen to those I had yet to visit.

Sometimes there was unfinished fishing boat business to be gone over when darkness fell on the quay. Some of it could be transacted around the bar in the White Hart or the Argyll Arms in Campbeltown. Duncan MacConnachie, my host at the Argyll, would keep coming to remind me that my 'tea' was waiting, and every time I had still two or three 'customers' expecting to discuss their problems. By the time I was through it would be nearly midnight; and Duncan would say that my supper was back in the hotel kitchen. There would be the 'works' waiting on the kitchen table – a mixed grill, with mushrooms and veg, and a sweet to follow. Next morning, when I asked for the overnight bill, the hotel receptionist handed me one for bed and breakfast only. I reminded her that I had had a sumptious supper the previous night and she would say, 'The boss told me not to charge you because it was all spoilt and dried up!'

I have focused on the more entertaining aspects of looking after the safety of fishing boats, mostly those of Tarbert and Kintyre; but under the surface of light-hearted and manly repartee, and little incidents which had to be winked at, there was a fairly solid ground of mutual trust, respect and concern for the life and limb of fishermen. While there were, perhaps, one or two exceptions to that attitude, there stand in my mind a multitude of highly professional, safety conscious and reliable skippers. To name only the few that I can readily remember, in Carradale, the MacConnachies of the *Florentine*, 'wee Jim' Campbell of *Bairn's Pride*, Colin Campbell of *Silver Fern*, Archie Paterson of *Harvest Queen*, Ronnie Brownie of the *Minerva*, later to become the *Scallop King* of Carradale, and last , but not least, 'Nonna' Campbell, in his day the grand old man of Carradale. In Campbeltown, James Meenan of *Stella Maris*, Neil Speed of *Moira*, Duncan MacArthur of *Mary Maclean*, Cecil Finn of the *Gleaner*. Amongst the 'Dookers' as Tarbert fishermen were known, there were John 'Tar' [pronounced Taar] MacDougall of *Nancy Glen*, 'Count' Jackson of the *Village Belle* and Robert Ross of the *Sunbeam*.

The Rothesay fishing fleet of the 1960s and '70s might have been smaller than the Kintyre fleets but it was vibrant and bristling with notable characters. There were the Hugheses – known as Shushies – brothers Tom, Jim and Willie Hughes of Port Bannatyne on the *Maid of the Mist*. I was told that the Hugheses, father Jimmy and the three sons, came to Rothesay early in the war from Pittenweem on the East Coast, which they had to leave because of the wartime fishing restrictions. They had a 57-ft Fifie and they acquired the *Maid of the Mist* in 1964. They were drift-netting men and they didn't take to ring-netting until they took on board a Campbeltown man, Bob Morans. The *Maid* was known to the citizens of Rothesay as the Sunday Post boat as she carried Sunday newspapers from the mainland and the *Sunday Post* of Oor Wullie and the Broons fame loomed large amongst them.

Tommy Rae's *Katheryn* was amongst the first prawn boats in the Firth of Clyde. Tommy Rae of Rothesay joined forces with the Marquis of Bute to start prawn processing. His son Tommy is still prawn creeling from Rothesay on his *Buccaneer*.

Jackie Alexander – sometime deputy harbourmaster of Rothesay – had *Teena*, a beautiful wee fishing vessel of sailing boat hull. He would not part with her until the oil rig works started in Ardyne and lured away fishing boat crews with big wages. Ardyne spelled a drastic diminution of the Rothesay fishing fleet.

Port Bannatyne skipper Jake McMillan on his *Marianne* once snagged a rope and was dragged overboard. When the crew fished him out he still had his pipe in his mouth and his first request was for a light for his pipe because it had gone out.

The Dougal brothers, came to Rothesay from Eyemouth on the East Coast early in the war on their *Guiding Star*. Along with Jock MacArthur on his *Sheina Glen*, they were the first in the late 1960s, to start dredging for 'queenie' scallops. This shallow-water species, small relatives of the clams, locally known as the creachans, were previously disregarded for lack of a market. When they were accidentally brought on board in a trawl they were often given away. I remember coming home from work one evening with a whole bag of throw-away creachans. My wife was not overjoyed to have them, she maintained that they 'winked' when cooked.

The two Rothesay fishermen, equipped with steel-toothed dredges, found such thick deposits of wee 'queenies' that they could fill thirty bags in one tow. Other boats followed using bobbin trawls with such success that by the early 1970s the species was almost fished out.

Of the small Gigha fishing fleet, the boat that lingers in my memory is the *Speedwell*, a Kelvin-engined lobster and clam boat. She was run for some fifteen years in the 1960s and '70s by that successful partnership of Ian Wilkieson and Graham MacCulloch. They were a friendly pair and must have regarded me also as a friend since at times, when inspecting equipment in their boat shed, a lemonade bottle would appear from under a coil of ropes, containing a fluid that might have been cold tea. Ian handed over his next scalloper *Girl Aileen* for a while to his son, John Ronald. At the time of writing he is being groomed to command the Lochranza–Claonaig ferry.

The fishing boats of the 1950s, '60s and '70s, I remember, were of wood construction, larch planking on oak frames, and of the traditional double-ended design. Many were built at Dickie's boatyard in Tarbert. The last such was was *Kirsteen Ann* for Eddy Laferty in 1967. The few steel boats that appeared in the early 1970s were sometimes the products of the resuscitated Campbeltown Shipyard. The first such was James Macdonald's *Crimson Arrow*, and one of the first was the 39-ft stern trawler/seine netter built for 'Cubby' Galbraith of Campbeltown. I well remember the jolly gathering in Campbeltown's White Hart Hotel following the launching. 'Cubby's' sister, the Mod Gold Medallist Carol [Galbraith] Thomson, having sung beautifully herself, quite kindly, if perversely, made us all sing with very varying effects.

The 1960s and '70s saw the culmination of a long process of changes in the fishing technique, particularly with regard to herring fishing. The time honoured system of drift-netting was first developed into trawling some time in the nineteenth century, partly because it was cheaper in boats and gear. Tarbert fishermen contrived, with considerable success, small trawls that consisted of several pieces of drift net attached to each other. A crew member would be landed with one end of the trawl and the boat would describe a circle and return to the shore with the other end. The landed crew would then pull at both ends until the net was hauled ashore. Perhaps because the new system was so successful it had to overcome violent opposition from conservative drift-netters. Ardrishaig men went with the Tarbert men, but the drift-net fishermen, north of Otter, in Upper Loch Fyne, were not in favour of 'trawling'. There were fierce battles up and down Loch Fyne between the trawlers and the drifters. Inveraray men would pitch the trawlers over the quay and the drifters from Upper Loch Fyne would be chased away as they came to Tarbert for the Fair in July. Islay men drove them out with ballast stones, 'Doirneag'. Brethren of Kintyre were treated as Capt. Cook's men were by the Polynesians. Trawling was made illegal by Act of Parliament in 1851 and remained so until 1867. A cruiser was stationed in Loch Fyne, guns would be fired into the air and torches waved at night to warn of the cruiser's approach. In Tarbert, barracks were erected to house the Fishery Police but the police tended to fraternise with the trawlers and men would contrive to sink the trawl nets to conceal them. However, one teenage Ardrishaig fisherman was shot dead and twenty-six Tarbert fishermen were at one time imprisoned in Campbeltown.

In time the herring got wise to the system and stopped coming close inshore. The fishermen had to start using two boats to describe a circle and hauling the net onto one boat instead of onto the shore. That is how ring-netting came about. It could be used in deeper waters and enabled

Campbeltown ring netters

the trapping of entire shoals in one ring and so avoided the hit-and-miss way of drifters, which had to rely on herring swimming into the drift-net. Ring-netting was worked in pairs, often referred to as 'neighbours'. The second boat completed the ring and provided buoyancy support when the weight of the ring bag being taken in made the first boat heel over. 'Neighbours' afloat were not always neighbours ashore; a Tarbert boat could be neighbour to a Campbeltown or a Carradale one. It was probably the most spectacular form of herring fishing but insufficiently efficient for these days and therefore has now been nearly abandoned altogether.

I have unforgettable memories of night fishing with the friendly John, James, Walter and Donald MacConnachies of Carradale on their *Florentine*, or with their 'neighbour' Jim Campbell on his *Bairn's Pride*. When peering ahead one saw that striking and startling phosphorescence that lit the sea with greeny brilliance in late summer and autumn. It was known as 'burning', or 'fire in the water'. It was produced by minute drifting plants of plankton when disturbed by movement of fish. One or two men had to take turns on the bow throughout the night, watching for the appearance of fish and intermittently 'chapping' with the anchor stock on the gunwale, as well as tapping or stamping. The sound wave so produced was expected to cause herring to start with a flash. This was

Carradale ring netters

referred to as 'answering the anchor'. John 'Shore' MacConnachie heard older men talk of seeing herring 'blue in the watter'. Then there was the magic circle of gold and silver when the ring had been described and most of the two boats' crews were floodlit in their orange oilskins on board the first boat hauling in the net of 'silver darlings', with the other boat giving support.

I could not leave the subject of ring-netters without a mention of the 'feeling wire'. The wire of anything up to 100 fathoms in length, with a lead weight at the end of it, usually wound round a fishbox, was still in my time used for exploring the nature of seabed in search of herring. It was used alongside such new equipment as echo-sounder and fish loop and continued in use for as long as ring-netting did. John MacConnachie of the *Florentine* once told me that when 'tapped' by sensitive and skilled hands the wire could out-achieve any electronic equipment.

In the late 1960s the Norwegian purse-seine arrived on the West Coast as a follow-up to the ring-net but many times the size of it. In a relatively short time it had brought the West Coast herring fishing nearly to an end. To give an idea of the dimensions and investment involved, at that time a standard ring net was about 200 yards long, 40 yards deep, carried about 250 lb of lead rings and cost about £1,000. Hence the investment in a sometimes ten times bigger purse-seine could amount to £10,000 sunk into gear, which turned out no longer to be needed in a relatively short period of time. Meanwhile, the Firth of Clyde was invaded by powerful pair-trawlers from the east coast and the north of Ireland. The fishermen of Tarbert, Carradale and Campbeltown were forced by these powerful competitors into pair-trawling and so had to upgrade their boats' engines from moderately powered Gardners and Perkinses to big Volvos and American Cummins engines. The outcome of this development turned out to be counter-productive because, as a result of pair-trawling having been taken up in the Firth of Clyde in the 1970s, by the '90s hardly a herring fisherman remained in that area.

The golden age of the Loch Fyne herring kipper has become a nostalgic memory and with it the renowned local characters associated with the Loch Fyne kipper trade. Such were Forsyth Hamilton of Ardrishaig, the gentleman 'Kipper King of Argyll'. Ardrishaig kippery was a regular port of call on my way home from Kintyre. Into the family-size consignment of kippers, Forsyth would, more often than not, squeeze a sample of salmon of his own smoking as a 'wee present for herself'. Another was wee Jimmy 'Jimpy' Richmond in Tarbert, whose wife used to sell his kippers from a close facing the Tarbert fish quay.

'Jimpy', when not involved in kippering, appeared as the odd job man at the Tarbert Hotel. One day, while I was anxiously waiting for an early breakfast at that hotel, not wanting to miss a morning assignment with a fishing boat, I was passing the time exchanging idle Tarbert gossip with 'Jimpy'. He was endeavouring to bring to life a dining-room fire with the help of a Calor gas cylinder. After a while I reminded one of the waitresses that I was ready for my early breakfast. She calmly assured me that I would have to go on waiting for it for as long as I went on blethering with 'Jimpy' and so preventing him from returning the hotel's one and only Calor gas cylinder to the kitchen.

In the early days of my surveying in the Firth of Clyde, daily catches by seine-netters were mainly of white fish. The odd and accidental catches of prawns were largely disregarded, just as scallop catches were. Just as with scallops, I would sometimes arrive home with a bagful of give-away prawns. My wife and I would have to spend half the night peeling them so as to give the neighbours a feast of fresh seafood next day.

The early 1960s were the golden years of Islay's lobster fishing. There were three big boats, our old friend Lachie Clark's 46-ft Weatherhead

Jim McFarlane's *Defiance II*

built ring-netter *May*, Tommy Epps' 35-ft *Belinda* and Jim McFarlane's 36-ft Orkney built *Defiance*. There were also six open boats on Islay's inshore grounds.

Lobsters were packed in tea chests with bracken, heather and sawdust, and sent to London by MacBrayne's and rail. Boxes were frequently pilfered so latterly they were dispatched by aircraft from Islay airport. Jim and Lachie landed their catches at Oban when aircraft couldn't cope. Lachie was a legend when it came to lobster fishing and many tales were told of his exploits from the Mull of Galloway to Cape Wrath. Once he landed a record catch of seventy boxes, equal to two and a half tons, after a short week's fishing from Kintyre. Lachie and Jim worked with wooden creels made with hazel bows, later changing to Tahiti cane. They claimed that wooden creels outfished steel, but admitted that maybe lobster was more plentiful in those days. Tommy Epps was the first to introduce steel-framed creels and a line hauler.

Tommy, for all he was reputed to have come from the East End of London, became just about the most successful tenant farmer of the Islay Estate. One could tell one was approaching the Gruinart farm by the juicy greenness the landscape would acquire. Having made a success of farming Tommy turned his versatile mind to fishing. He got himself a 35-ft catamaran for creeling in the shallow loch and in time became a major lobster exporter from Islay. Tommy contrived a lobster pond within the confines of Loch Gruinart. It became so well stocked that there was talk on Islay of Tommy letting some lobster out on parole on the understanding that they would come home before Christmas when prices were at their best.

Tommy Epps had a habit of being in several places at once and communicating with him was not easy. This is where Islay's angelic lady telephone operators would come to the rescue. One day I left Gilbert Clark's wee boatyard at Port Charlotte, and headed for the telephone box on the pier. Gilbert was Lachie's cousin and builder of the renowned Lochindaal skiffs. When I asked to be put through to Tommy Epps, Flora, the young lady telephone operator, reminded me that it being Wednesday, Tommy was, of course, shopping in Bowmore and that afterwards he had a long-distance call booked. She could however give him a message from me. And so Flora arranged for Tommy to meet me at his wee Loch Gruinart jetty at nine o'clock the next morning; and having been spared the next hour's waiting in a rain-drenched telephone box, I could retire to the Port Charlotte Hotel for a refreshment.

When I asked Bella, the other kind-hearted soul operating the Islay exchange, to put me through to John Mackay at Portnahaven she did not even hesitate on account of John not having a phone. She simply called the Fergusons, his neighbours, to send a lad to fetch him and to ring me back. I have nostalgic memories of the islands' benevolent telephone ladies who were guardian angels, social workers and citizens' advice bureaux rolled into one.

Effy MacDougall, who operated Jura's exchange for many years, admirably fitted all those roles. She not only kept Jura people informed of how late the MacBrayne ferry would be arriving at the Small Isles but also of who would be on board. Her wee whisper advising of the presence on board of a visiting constable would chase most of the island's cars into their owner's gardens, just in case it got into the officer's head to check the vehicles' registration discs.

Effy was due to retire in the early 1970s. While I was sitting at the Craighouse Hotel bar in the company of Dan MacDougall the Jura piermaster, it struck me that he might give me some ideas on a suitable retirement present for her. I asked him for advice on that matter. He took another sip of the Laphroaig, scratched his head and was not hurrying

Islay Scallop fishery. Top: *Argonaut*; Centre: *Bonnie Lass*; Bottom: *Cynasure*

with his reply. After a lengthy consideration of my problem he advised me slowly and deliberately that the best thing I could do for Effy was to buy him another large dram as he was her husband. Effy's retirement present somehow fell by the wayside that time, but twenty-five years later, when I happened to be on Jura once again, I knocked on Effy's door bearing a large box of chocolates, a retirement present delayed by a quarter of a century! Needless to say I was graciously received by that gracious lady.

Coming now to scallop fishing, or dredging, from Islay takes me back in my memory to one summer in the late 1960s when a whole fleet of scallop boats from the Isle of Man descended on the Isle of Islay where I happened to be paying one of my periodic duty visits. Apparently Isle of Man had imposed a six months' ban, from May to November, to conserve stocks. It seems to have worked; stock there is still healthy more than forty years on! I found that none of the visitors had the safety equipment of UK registered vessels of similar dimensions. They protested that Manx laws don't call for meeting the same standards and were told that while fishing in UK waters and competing with UK fishermen they had to follow UK rules. In consequence, to the delight of Islay fishermen, their boats were detained in Port Ellen until they acquired and installed the missing gear. In the following evenings a wee queue of Manx skippers and second hands would form in the tiny porch of my billet at Sheila MacEwan's at Port Ellen. They carried newly acquired lifebuoys, distress rockets, lifejackets and fire extinguishers, making the first step towards having their boats released from detention.

My landlady Sheila MacEwan became quite adept at recognising from across the harbour which boat was due to be visited. She would wake me up with a call to look through my bedroom window for the red boat in the distance. 'Get yourself down for your porridge', she would command, 'Then quickly make your way round the harbour to the wee red boat. By the time you have done with her, I'll have your bacon and egg ready.' People started referring to Sheila as the honorary Board of Trade surveyor for Port Ellen.

Reverting to the Manx invasion of Islay, one has to grant that the two scallop processing plants on Islay were founded by Manx enterprises and provided good employment on the island. Islay fishermen soon joined the action. After 1965 small lobster boats were replaced by 40-ft scallop boats at Port Ellen. Over the next ten years the fleet increased in size and numbers. In turn, the 40-ft boats were being replaced by 55-ft boats, seeking scallops further afield, the local grounds having been fished out.

Islay boats were venturing north to Barra, Skye and Tiree. Islay Scallop Gear, run by an Islay ex-fisherman, was supplying boats from all over the British Isles with a type of equipment called Oban scallop gear. Men and boys were desperate for a berth on any boat. Young men out of school were making big money, driving new cars and thinking they'd never be poor again!

The scallop boom lasted till 1985. It was slowly declining as boats became bigger and more efficient. Modern electronic gear, satellite navigation and track plotters took their toll. At the time of writing four scallop boats remain in Port Ellen. Most men have gone back to small day boats, fishing for velvet crabs. Boats are working single handed, or at the most with two men.

For a parting shot on leaving Islay, I quote an Islay friend about the three Islay fishermens' reactions to the Board of Trade Man discovering Islay in the 1960s: Jim McFarlane – 'Another Obstacle.' Tom Epps – 'We have to comply.' Lachie Clark – 'Och, the man is only human. A wee back hander will do.'

There was only one Tiree fisherman I knew, and that was Hector MacPhail, who died in his fifties in 1997. I cannot do better than to let Douglas Rolland, his friend, and himself a fisherman, tell us about him.

> My first encounter with Hector was during our first trip to Tiree, fishing lobster and velvet crab. With no vessel in sight, my VHF radio exploded into life one morning, 'Boat from Crinan, what are you fishing here?' the powerful voice demanded. Terrified that we might be boarded by locals and ritually disembowelled for fishing in Tiree waters, I feebly responded that we were fishing buckies (whelks, then unmarketable), but my apprehension was misplaced. Hector's bark was loud, but he was more interested than critical. In time, Hector became a firm ally and along with his esteemed brother-in-law, Iain MacDonald (of the FV *Kohoutec*), we assisted each other in times of need. One fresh December afternoon our gearbox packed in close to shore off Vaul, North Tiree. The coastguard alerted Hector and Iain who gladly came to our rescue, towing us to safety. On our next trip out, I left a quantity of whisky for my friends. We met up with Iain and shared drams, but after several months, I was curious that Hector hadn't acknowledged its receipt. At length I enquired if he'd got the drams, 'Oh . . . aye, but if it had been the other way round, you'd have got bugger all!' and walked off. Truth was, conventional niceties could be irrelevant to Hector, co-operation on the high seas was what was rightly taken for granted.

Hector built his reputation as a skilled, intrepid fisherman whose intimate knowledge of the waters was second to none. Iain MacDonald recalls how Hector took his *Harvest Home* in tow when broken down round Hynish Point through the tidal reefs with his *Alice Robert* of eight feet draft. An achievement in daylight, but this was in the dark! And at full speed!

Hector was keenly interested in people and their stories from the past and present. His story telling was compelling, if not theatrical. Customarily relaxed in demeanour, when regaling a company, he'd quite dominate the gathering by his physical presence, which seemed to grow as his yarn progressed. His deep, articulate tones demanded attention, at first slow and subdued, then, developing his theme, his voice would boom, his eyes flash and as he reached a crescendo, wild gesticulating arms and unruly hair heightened the drama further. His 'performances" were legendary, but this wasn't acting, this was just Hector.

I recall him in full flow aboard my boat *Zolee* embellishing a tale about creeling at St Kilda by seizing our long bait knife and plunging the blade repeatedly and with relish into the top of the baiting table until the story's drama had subsided. His style was consistent, whether addressing a ceilidh, or bumping into a fisherman mending creels at the pier on his own. As an audience of one, I felt privileged, if not a little frightened!

Hector, colourful, creative, imaginative, inspiring, philosophical, at times outrageous, and always totally memorable. On the 'dreichest' fishing day when the perpetual aggravation of a restless, slopping sea wearied the stoutest limbs and the lack of crabs depressed the stoutest heart, even then, to listen to the gospel according to Hector over the boat's radio was enough to raise a smile and spirits, until the day was done.

No defender of bullshit or bureaucracy, Hector was an able campaigner, lobbying and applying for grants to build a new pier at Acarsaid (the Harbour Caolas, Tiree). His years at sea and with different people had taught him the tough realities of life. Forces greater than man can menace you, toy with you, destroy you. To reach harbour safely after days at sea is about more than earning a living, it's about survival, bringing your crew and boat home, in one piece. If there's money to share, all well and good.

Latterly Hector worked for the Tiree and Coll Gaelic partnership collecting information on families, careers of Tiree people throughout the world, and, of course, old stories. Happily, Hector's own life story is as remarkable as any, reflecting a life of adventure, love and fulfilment. His memory will be cherished by all who knew him.

Flora, Hector's widow, a teacher, remains as the guiding spirit of Tiree. She is the fountainhead of Tiree tradition, history, enthusiasm and good humour. Hector's son Neil is a fisherman and has had his own boat since he was nineteen. His younger brother Angus is a piper and an accordionist. He is musical in boatmanship!

I cannot conclude reflecting on the fishing scene of the West Coast of Scotland in the 1960s and '70s without saying a few words about the 'Scottish Navy' of the day. That was the name colloquially bestowed upon the small fleet of fishery protection vessels directed by the Agriculture and Fishery Department of St Andrews House in Edinburgh.

The oldest of that fleet was the *Ulva*, a wartime built Island Class trawler/patrol vessel, propelled by a coal-fired steam engine. *Ulva*'s speed was somewhat less that that of an average Firth of Clyde seine-netter or trawler and the plume of black smoke she used to emit was visible from a long distance. This enabled any offending fishing boat to keep well out of her way. *Ulva* used to be responsible for patrolling the Firth of Clyde. While on summer holiday at Catacol on the west shore of Arran in those days, I could set my watch by the tell-tale black emission, somewhere in Kilbranan Sound, passing Catacol Bay at 5 p.m. It may have been a coincidence that *Ulva* was timed to arrive back at her base in Campbeltown just before 'opening time'!

New fishery protection vessels were purpose built soon after the war by Denny of Dumbarton. *Brenda* and *Minna* were followed by *Freya* about 1960. *Freya* encountered severe weather in the Pentland Firth right at the beginning of her service and capsized with the tragic loss of her master, Captain McLaren. He went down with the ship, still in her wheelhouse from which he could not escape, because the sliding door had jammed.

In the course of the investigation that ensued, and in which I was involved, it was found that the shipyard designers slipped up in preparing hydrostatic curves for these ships by neglecting the fact that they were intended to operate at a permanent trim by the stern of 4 feet. The result was a very reduced reserve of stability. *Brenda* and *Minna* had to be called into Greenock one at a time and have their reserve of buoyancy increased by constructing longer superstructures, and so restoring a reserve of stability.

All in all, the 'Scottish Navy' of those days, in spite of these and the other shortcomings of its vessels, had an honourable record. Manned by dedicated and competent seamen, she contributed in no small measure to slowing down the reduction of fish stocks around Scottish coasts in that period.

4

SINKING OF THE *QUESADA* AND THE
CAPSIZE OF THE *ISLE OF GIGHA*

The event that made Campbeltown my home-from-home for a while was the loss of the *Quesada*.

The *Quesada* was built in 1937 by British Power Boats of Hythe in the Solent as a 58-ft twin-motor minesweeper of wooden double diagonal 'chine' construction, and therefore rather flat-bottomed. She was converted in 1939 to a motor torpedo boat powered by three hefty Napier engines, and between 1956 and 1960 was made into a pleasure craft in Cornwall with two somewhat less powerful Dorman engines.

In 1963 she found her way to a garage proprietor and second-hand car dealer of Scone in Scotland. He, in turn, sold her to Campbeltown and

Portside view of the *Quesada*

by the spring of 1966 she was owned and sailed by John Macmillan. John had just lost his *Crammond Brig*, which he had operated with so-called 'charter parties' of passengers, by stranding at Torrisdale Point early in 1966. My attention was drawn to Mr John Macmillan's operations by the then Campbeltown harbourmaster, Captain Hugh MacShannon.

It so happened I was in Campbeltown in mid-April of that year in order, among other inspections, to survey the *Heather*, John MacMillan's brother Alec's boat. I looked up John on the *Quesada* and proposed to him that her hull and machinery should be surveyed for the issue of a passenger certificate if he carried more that twelve passengers and a load line certificate if not more than twelve were carried. John maintained that, carrying 'charter parties', *Quesada* could be classed as a yacht and therefore required only safety equipment appropriate to the yacht class. He wrote down a list of required safety equipment items I gave him, which included twelve life-jackets, an inflatable life-raft for twelve and six red star distress rockets. Mr MacMillan was to get in touch with me when all the equipment was available for inspection. His letter did not reach my office until the morning after Sunday 22 May, the day of the fateful cruise.

On that morning, *Quesada* sailed from Campbeltown with eighteen on board. They were mostly a party from Neil Patterson's garage organised by his son John, plus two farmers. The crew consisted of the owner-skipper John MacMillan, 'Baldie' Stewart, a 76-year-old retired fisherman, John MacCallum a marine engineer, Archie Gillies, a radio engineer and Kenneth Copping, a 15-year-old sea cadet. The remaining thirteen paid fifty shillings each for the trip.

The original intention was to cross to Northern Ireland but because of ominous weather forecasts it was decided to sail up the Firth of Clyde instead. They called at Lochranza for 'elevenses' at the Lochranza Hotel. That afternoon, by coincidence, I saw them in Rothesay harbour, as I happened to be staying on the island of Bute for the month of May with my young family. The crew and passengers seemed to be in high spirits, singing and playing the bagpipes. I saw *Quesada* again later that evening, at dusk, while watching over my young sons and their friends scrambling on the cliffs overlooking Dunegoil Bay. As she came out of the sheltered waters of the Kyles of Bute she appeared to have been laid on her beam by the northwesterly wind which must have been about Force 6 gusting to Force 8. I was hoping that she would put into Carradale for shelter, but sadly she didn't.

From that point on, the story is based on statements taken in the course of the inquiry. Following the Kintyre coastline southwards, the boat suffered some slamming and an occasional shudder and a list to port but there was no ominous behaviour and the vessel benefited from the weather shore while the wind rose to Force 8 northwesterly. It was only when she passed Otterard Buoy and picked up the leading lights of Campbeltown Harbour, a little less than half a mile north east of Davaar Light, that 'Baldie' Stewart at *Quesada*'s helm experienced a difficulty in steering the boat to starboard and keeping her on a southwesterly course.

The port engine had stopped and steerage way was lost about forty minutes past midnight. The vessel was being carried by her starboard engine to the east and south of Davaar Island. John MacMillan went down into the engine room to find it partly flooded. He was overcome by what might have been exhaust fumes and he had to be helped up. It became very stormy as the vessel lost the lee of Kintyre shore. Archie Gillies sent out a mayday call and it was received by Arran Coastguard at 0053 hours. The first flare was lit within seconds of the commencement of the mayday message and was seen off the southern tip of Davaar just as Kildonan radio was acknowledging *Quesada*'s mayday message. While mayday was still being broadcast eleven life-jackets were being handed out. This was seven short of the eighteen persons on board. It was established that John MacMillan had ordered ten approved-type lifejackets and these had been delivered in good time to the Campbeltown ship chandlers, but had not been collected before departure. Twelve red star distress rockets had also been ordered and delivered but not collected. Of the five hand flares that were used, only the first and the last were seen, the rest were obscured by Davaar Island. No inflatable life-raft was on board. John MacMillan had ordered one from Beauforts but they weren't able to supply it. There was on board an old-fashioned Buoyant Apparatus, i.e. a rigid life-raft with lifelines all round it, and there were also three lifebuoys with one self-igniting light.

At about 0100 hours, as all men were assembled on the foredeck, the starboard engine stopped and lights went out due to flooding of the entire engine room. The radio telephone was put out of action as the 12-volt batteries in the forward accommodation were submerged. The vessel's stability was destroyed by the large free surface inside and she was listing heavily, as much as 35° now to port and then to starboard as the wind caught her on either side. At the same time she was being driven by a Force 9 northwesterly gale in the general direction of Ailsa Craig with speed steadily reduced by the submergence of the exposed area as the stern went down. The atmosphere on board was fairly calm, largely due to the reassuring behaviour of John MacMillan and Jack MacCallum. John asked for the life-raft lashings to be cut and four men were holding on to it.

Suddenly the boat lurched right over to starboard and stayed in that position. It was then that the four men holding on to the life-raft and two others were thrown overboard. The remainder, probably eleven, climbed onto the port side and held on to the port bulwark. The twelfth, 'Baldie' Stewart, who wanted to hold on to his little dog as long as possible, remained on the foredeck and he lashed himself to the anchor davit.

About the time *Quesada* went over on her starboard side the lights of the rescue vessel were first spotted rounding Davaar Light. John MacMillan then lit the last flare with the help of a cigarette; Jack MacCallum was managing to smoke while lying on the ship's side. It was 0110 hours when the rescue boat saw the flare. There followed about half an hour of waiting on the wreck while the rescuers made their way towards it. Jack MacCallum was singing the hymn 'Rock of Ages' and so kept everyone calm. He was lost as the rescue boat *Moira* rounded the wreck's bow, perhaps when going forward to board her. As the *Moira* approached she was helped in locating the wreck by a flicker from Lamont Conley's lighter. Jim Meenan on *Moira* counted eleven people on the wreck as John MacMillan was still on board. It seems that he might have been lost while attempting to climb the *Moira*'s side at the foremost and highest part of her sheer. It is doubtful whether he had kept a life jacket for himself and was last seen floating face down. It took *Moira* about half an hour to haul ten survivors on board and it was about 0200 hours when the last of them, 'Baldie' Stewart was rescued.

The saga of *Quesada*'s rescue began with Neil Patterson, whose son John organised the outing. The weather conditions were so severe that general anxiety was felt for the safety of the boat, which carried eighteen of Campbeltown's citizens. Over and above that, Neil Patterson felt a little anxiety about the performance of *Quesada*, in which he had sailed to Northern Ireland the previous weekend. He got in touch with Southend Coastguard. They, having been unsuccessful in locating *Quesada*, advised Campbeltown lifeboat honorary secretary Tony MacGrory to launch at 0017 hours. Tony didn't want to send the lifeboat on a wild goose chase and tried first to satisfy himself that *Quesada* was on her way home from Rothesay. Having so satisfied himself, at 0031 hours the honorary secretary alerted by telephone the mechanic, the assistant secretary, the coxswain and the second coxswain. He then heard that John's brother Alec had seen the *Quesada* proceeding down the coast from Carradale and delayed the order to fire maroons. However, about the same time, 0053 hours, *Quesada*'s first flare was seen over the Dhorlin and Norman Wheeler telephoned to say that he had heard the mayday call on his radio. The first maroon went off at 0100 hours. The coxswain, the first mechanic and others were ferrying themselves to the lifeboat and Neil Patterson collected the second mechanic and the bowman. By 0120 hours the lifeboat was halfway down Campbeltown Loch.

In the meantime, in Campbeltown Harbour, James Meenan skipper of *Stella Maris*, Duncan MacArthur skipper of *Mary MacLean* and Neil Speed skipper of *Moira*, all on board *Moira*, saw the red flare over the Dhorlin and shortly after that heard the first maroon. Those three with Archie Galbraith and three others on board the *Moira* started for *Quesada* about 0055 hours. They cleared Davaar lighthouse about 0110 hours, and at 0130, half a mile off the wreck, they saw the flicker of Lamont Conley's lighter and a few minutes later were picking up survivors. They executed a most skilful manoeuvre by coming alongside *Quesada* on the port side round the wreck's bow into the wind and then, by bringing *Moira* hard to starboard over the wreck's sunken stern, allowed the wind to do the rest, i.e. to take the *Moira* diagonally across *Quesada*, bear down on the wreck's superstructure and so wedge herself against it. In this way, the two boats were made to drift together and all hands on the *Moira* were free for rescue work. According to one survivor the manoeuvre was carried out with such apparent ease that all he could remember was a gentle grinding of timbers. See diagram opposite.

The rescue work itself required an almost superhuman effort as the men were heavy, the *Moira* very high and the wreck very low in the water. And the rescuers had nothing to put their backs against because a fishing boat's bulwarks are very low. The fishermen found the survivors orderly and calm and some tried to help as soon as they got on board.

The lifeboat was, in starting, only ten minutes behind the *Moira*, but the lag increased to fifteen minutes due to her slower speed. The lifeboat arrived at the wreck at 0150 hours just as the *Moira*'s men, having rescued nine off the *Quesada*, found themselves in difficulty over getting a line across to 'Baldie' Stewart, still on the bow of the wreck. There followed a long exchange of radio messages between *Moira* and the lifeboat, but in the end it was *Moira* that got the tenth man, 'Baldie' Stewart, on board.

Moira rescue diagram

During the rescue operation, the lifeboat remained to the lee of *Moira* and the wreck and later proceeded downwind at a speed of two to three knots, which was the expected speed of the missing life-raft drifting. They fetched up between Ailsa Craig and Pladda and continued searching till 1440 hours on Monday 23 May. In fact, the empty life-raft was found by a fisherman at 0600 hours only 1½ miles to lee of the sinking. Obviously wind had had little effect on the life-raft. The three skippers in their respective boats and other fishermen searched till the afternoon of the 23rd. A Shackleton aircraft from Kinloss appeared on the scene and started searching at 0400 hours on Monday 23rd.

I heard of the casualty on the eight o'clock radio news while about to leave my Isle of Bute holiday home for my Greenock office. That day, I was appointed by the Board of Trade headquarters to carry out a Preliminary Inquiry into the casualty. Next day, early in the morning, I headed for Campbeltown to meet, in the first place, Inspector Donald Macleod who was heading the police investigation on behalf of the Procurator Fiscal. To start with he advised me to make my base in the Argyll Arms Hotel because, of the other two, the Royal was owned by Archie Malcolm, the lifeboat coxswain, and Mrs Copping, mother of the teenager lost with the *Quesada*, was working at the White Hart.

There followed weeks devoted to investigations and taking statements which led me to:

1 establish the cause of the casualty;
2 assess the effectiveness of the rescue operation;
3 find who was responsible;

As regards the first, I found that the most likely primary cause was the failure of the port exhaust discharge just above the waterline. The boat was proceeding along the Kintyre coast listing to port under the force of the northwesterly gale. The submerging of the port side had put the exhaust's skin fitting under considerable pressure and produced a shudder. That and the slamming of the after-body would fracture the dry exhaust pipe weakened by corrosion caused by high temperatures and corrosive fumes and accelerated by the injection of salt water. Supporting this conclusion was a statement by the previous owner of *Quesada* that the exhaust pipe had not been renewed during the three-year period of his ownership, a statement he later denied. The fact that John MacMillan was temporarily overcome, possibly by exhaust fumes, when he went down to the engine room after the port engine stopped, could also be construed as supporting that conclusion. Finally, the 3-inch diameter opening resulting from the dislodging of the exhaust pipe was, according to my calculations, consistent with the speed of flooding of the engine compartment.

The most obvious way to justify my conclusion would have been either to salvage the wreck and examine the port exhaust fitting or to carry out an underwater inspection of it. To that effect, I had obtained the services of skipper Cecil Finn who, with his fishing boat *Gleaner*'s gear, had managed to snag an underwater object that seemed to be at the right location and of the right length. I then persuaded the management of the Naval Salvage Depot in Greenock that using the salvage vessel *Succour* for the salvage of *Quesada* would be a most useful exercise for them. The *Succour* duly arrived and anchored at the indicated spot about 4½ miles south-east of Davaar Island. A diver was sent down, located the sunken object and came up with a sample of it which was a broken-off piece of an aluminium structure. The wreck was more likely the remains of a wartime German bomber than the *Quesada*.

Thus I still had the task of presenting the Court of Inquiry that sat in Campbeltown Sheriff Court in November 1966 with the case for the port exhaust being the primary cause of the disaster. The secondary cause seemed to be the barely protected entrance to the saloon. Had the saloon not been flooded from the deck it would probably have retained sufficient buoyancy to keep the *Quesada* afloat because the engine room bulkhead, having been built to Admiralty standards, was watertight.

In order to present the best case for the port exhaust theory it would have been helpful if the court, consisting of the Sheriff and two professional assessors, had been more sceptical about the previous owner's (a second-hand car dealer) denial of his first statement, which meant that the exhaust pipe had 4½ years in which to corrode rather than 18 months. This witness appeared in court during a morning session. Later, during lunch with the Sheriff and assessors, I was dismayed to hear that the witness had appeared to them to be a most reliable and trustworthy one.

There was some quick thinking to be done to reinforce my proposition to the court that the dry steel exhaust pipe could have corroded to the point of fracture in 18 months. What I needed was a second expert opinion and for that purpose I got in touch with Donald MacIntyre, a boatyard and garage owner and manager of Port Bannatyne on Bute, and in the name of our old friendship persuaded him to appear before the court at short notice and give his opinion. While the witness was replying to questions put to him by Donald MacNiven, the incomparable solicitor for the Board of Trade, I was sitting helpless and praying that the witness would not complicate the issue and say no more than to corroborate my proposition.

As regards the rescue operation, I put before the court a commendation for the rescuers on board the *Moira*, for their skill, courage and superhuman effort and especially for Neil Speed, *Moira*'s skipper and Neil Meenan who directed the operation. In fact those two, or at least one and the widow of the other, were the following year presented with special awards by Mr Mallalieu, Minister of Shipping in Harold Wilson's government, who arrived for that purpose at Machrahanish airport in a ministerial executive jet.

When it came to responsibility, one couldn't avoid blame being attached to John MacMillan's carelessness in not having the boat equipped for the purpose although it is not certain that, had he done so, all the eight lives would have been saved. However, I put before the court that both the crew and passengers of *Quesada* acted like men to the last, that there was no panic and no selfish behaviour. Of the crew, John MacMillan, Jack MacCallum, Archie Gillies and 'Baldie' Stewart had not availed themselves of any of the eleven available life jackets and the youngest on board, Kenneth Copping, was given both a life jacket and a lifebuoy. By all accounts, Jack MacCallum showed outstanding gallantry and John MacMillan acted as a calm and considerate skipper and the last hour of his life was not unworthy.

There were a few lessons that could have been learned from the casualty and one was that, in spindrift conditions, a rigid life-raft, life jackets and lifebuoys do not necessarily guarantee survival and that the best chance for it may be to stick to the wreck as long as possible.

In the end I succeeded in my proposition to the court that the most likely cause of *Quesada*'s loss was a fracture of the port exhaust. And so on 11 November 1966, on conclusion of the Court of Inquiry, I was stepping down from the Campbeltown Sheriff Court, quite pleased with myself, when Norman Wheeler stopped me and reminded me that a piece of salmon was waiting for me in his deep freeze. I followed him to his house and, just as we were partaking of a 'wee refreshment', the telephone rang. It was the driver of a MacConnochie's bus, on his way from Tarbert, calling from a public box somewhere near Tayinloan asking for the Board of Trade surveyor. He thought that the surveyor might like to know that he had seen a barge capsizing off the Churne Islands. The barge turned out to be the new vehicular ferry *Isle of Gigha* and so another casualty inquiry started at once. But that is another story. However, how was that for another example of the Kintyre bush telegraph in action.

The ferry *Isle of Gigha* was the brainchild of a civil engineer by the name of John Rose who happened also to be a merchant seaman with a foreign-going mate's certificate. He lived in Oban and came to a not unreasonable view that the Western Isles of Scotland could do with vehicle-carrying ferries. With this in mind he got Gavin Hamilton, a Lanarkshire landscape gardener, to join him in approaching first boat-builders, and then the Highlands and Islands Development Board. From the Thames Launch Works they got a design that the boatyard used and advertised, and the Board promised them a grant. Then in February 1966, jointly with Chris Pollock, a limekiln owner of Clachan, Argyll, they formed a company called Eilean Sea Services.

In order to expedite the construction, Thames Launch Works entrusted the building to Bideford Shipyard and such was the haste that the craft was half built before the structural plans were submitted for approval to the Board of Trade Plymouth office.

Thames Launch Works, the principal contractors and construction supervisors, influenced no doubt by a late delivery penalty clause, were spurring on the subcontractors. In consequence the building was completed in record time but the attention paid to compliance with the plans was not very exacting, particularly with regard to the rudder assembly, avoidance of discontinuities, etc. Welding of some critical joints, such as that of the rudder-stock to coupling plates, seemed to have been done in a bit of a hurry. John Alban of Thames Launch Works was to sanction any departure from the plans but he did it only once.

The vessel, an 80-ft landing craft, in effect a square pontoon with shaped bow and stern, was handed over to the owners in May 1966. They were not entirely satisfied with the performance and stability trials and yet they accepted the ship and delivered her under her own power from Bideford to Loch Sween. Apparently she behaved quite well on that voyage.

A few weeks after the *Isle of Gigha* started working in the Inner Isles trade it became apparent that the after-peak tank was not holding water due to shell fractures. There followed a prolonged and inconclusive exchange of correspondence between John Alban and John Rose and sporadic and ineffective welding attempts at sealing the fractures on beaches at Oban.

In the course of the summer of 1966 the ship took on a fairly regular trading pattern, mostly between West Loch Tarbert or Tayinloan and Gigha or Islay. Beach landings, sometimes in gale force winds, took quite a heavy toll of her hull, resulting in more shell fractures and jamming of the port rudder. The crew were under constant instruction to sound tanks before commencing each voyage, and particularly after each grounding. This apparently could not be done in practice because the sounding pipe caps were almost permanently seized. Often the only means the crew had of checking the contents of the tanks was pumping them. This meant pumping air on some occasions, burning out impellers and in effect depriving the vessel of pumping capacity.

Neither the owners nor the builders appeared to be concerned about the vessel operating in an unseaworthy condition in the autumn, still less with the winter weather approaching. While the owners' requests to John Alban, the builder's director, for dry-docking repairs to the ship met with stonewalling, it didn't occur to them to stop the ship sailing until such repairs were done. Chris Pollock, the third director of the owning company, resigned from the board partly on those grounds. He was

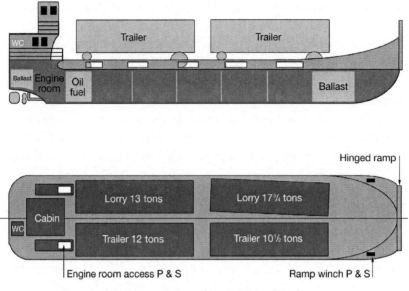

Elevation and plan of loaded *Isle of Gigha*

also unhappy because the managing director did not pass to the skipper weather restrictions issued by the Board of Trade because, 'they would prejudice the skipper's professional judgement'.

In the evening of 10 November 1966 the ship was loaded at Tayinloan ramp with two trailers on the starboard side and two lorries on the port side. The total load was 53 tons and the load on port side was 8 tons greater than on the starboard side. This was counteracted by one of the lorries on port side being angled towards the centreline. None of the vehicles was lashed, although deck rings were available for that purpose. It is not certain how many of the steel wheels of the trailers had wooden pads inserted under them, nor how many pneumatic wheels were choked.

That night the skipper Gordon Graham, accompanied by the lorry drivers, took the ship-single handed from Tayinloan to Gigha. At Gigha he was joined by Michael MacNeill, a native of Gigha, an ex-Glasgow assistant harbourmaster and an experienced seaman, who was to act as a deckhand. They left at 8.15 a.m. bound for Port Ellen, steered round the south end of Gigha, taking the passage inside Cara and then heading almost in a westerly direction. The moderate sea was on the ship's port bow and with the wind a southwesterly Force 4 to 5, she was riding kindly to it, albeit with some movement.

At about 9.15 a.m., when the ship came out into open sea, she began to roll heavily to the wind. The skipper decided then to hand the helm over to the deckhand. He wanted first to check the engine injectors, which were giving trouble, and then to start lashing the deck cargo. While he was in the engine room, a wave struck the vessel on her port beam and half the load of the forward trailer slipped off to starboard. It was hanging over the side, held only by tarpaulins. The ship took a lurch to starboard just as the skipper was coming up the engine room ladder, and she took up a list of between 15° and 20°.

The next wave caused the forward lorry to shift to starboard into the space vacated by the trailer. The skipper then brought the ship into the wind but he could not keep her hove to. Next he asked the driver of the port forward lorry to move back into position, but before any attempt could be made to do so another wave struck, increasing the list and bringing the starboard deck edge under water. The deckhand was told to set off distress signals, but as he reached for them the vessel took her final plunge and capsized to starboard. The skipper escaped through the port wheelhouse window.

Donald Macleod, the master of the MacBrayne's motor-ship *Lochiel*, and his mate John Carswell sighted the *Isle of Gigha* approaching at three points on their starboard, on a westerly course. She was about half a mile due north when she came abeam at 9.45 a.m., had a list of about 15° and was steering erratically. A few minutes later they saw the ferry about two miles south of the Chuirne Islands trying to keep her head into the wind and capsizing to starboard. The *Lochiel* was ordered to steer on reverse course and proceed to rescue.

When the *Lochiel* came abreast the casualty, the motor lifeboat on her starboard side was lowered with three men and the chief officer in charge. One of the drivers, who could swim and who hung on to a piece of timber from his own lorry, was taken aboard the lifeboat. The other driver, who could not swim, drifted out of reach of the other man and by the time the lifeboat was lowered was floating face down. The skipper held on to an empty drum for a few minutes and when the *Lochiel* came towards him climbed on board through the starboard shell door. He last saw the deckhand Michael MacNeill clinging to the starboard side of the wheelhouse and was presumably trapped under the wreck. Just as the two survivors came on board, Captain Macleod's mayday call was received by Oban Radio and, via Kilchonan Coastguard, the honorary secretary of the Islay Lifeboat. This resulted in the lifeboat being launched at Port Askaig at 10.36 a.m. When she approached the upturned hull the coxswain noticed that one of the rudders was in a fore-and-aft, and the other in an athwartship, position. The Islay lifeboat took over the search from the *Lochiel*'s lifeboat. HMS *Murray* arrived on the scene some two hours later and sent divers to inspect the wreck underwater. Neither of the two missing men was found alive. The *Lochiel* took the survivors to West Loch Tarbert, and arrived at that pier at 3 p.m.

While the search and rescue was going on at sea, I, in Campbeltown, acting on the 'bush telegraph' message, phoned Coastguard Southend and found that the 'barge' was the *Isle of Gigha*. I headed for West Loch Tarbert pier in the company of Mr Braund, a treasury solicitor, and we arrived there just as the *Lochiel* came alongside. Mr Braund later took part in the *Isle of Gigha* Court of Inquiry.

We were able to take preliminary depositions from Captains Gordon Graham and Donald Macleod, this being probably a unique personal participation of a treasury solicitor in a preliminary, on-the-spot, inquiry into a marine casualty. My own appointment to carry out the enquiry came by phone from the Board of Trade headquarters that afternoon. The surviving driver was not in a fit condition to be interviewed at that time.

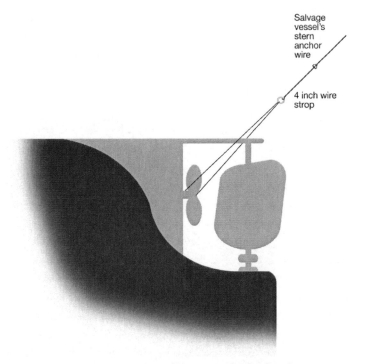

Towing arrangements for upturned *Isle of Gigha*

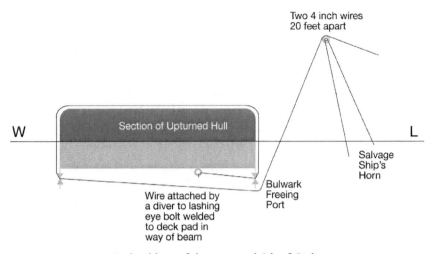

Parbuckling of the upturned *Isle of Gigha*

There were some dozen national and Scottish newspaper reporters at the pier. They followed us, having attended the *Quesada* court of inquiry in Campbeltown. Most of them I knew, and could persuade not to interview anyone concerned until I had taken down their statements. They co-operated well on the whole.

The Admiralty salvage vessel *Succour* arrived on the scene in the afternoon of the same day. The first attempt at securing a 2¼ inch flexible steel wire strop around the starboard propeller shaft and skeg ended in the tow carrying away. It seems that the wire slipped from the skeg to the rudder-stock and the towing pull made the stock jump out of the skeg bearing. At this point the unsupported stock broke off due to the bending load imposed on it. The result was intact strop and shackle and a lost starboard rudder. When a 2½ inch strop was secured over the port propeller shaft and skeg, (see sketch) the ship was successfully towed into the shelter of Proaig Bay on the east side of Islay. On the morning of 12 November *Succour* righted the hull by parbuckling, as shown on the sketch, and she towed it to Greenock where I could go over the hull afloat.

During the following days and weeks I was busy taking depositions on oath from the relevant witnesses. It was not always a simple task and sometimes quite a prolonged one. One of the witnesses to be interviewed was Donnie, the coxswain of the Islay lifeboat. I spent two days in Tarbert waiting for the weather to moderate sufficiently for the *Loch Nevis* to venture to Port Ellen. The usual *Lochiel* was undergoing dry-docking. On the third day I arrived at Port Ellen and was conveyed by bus to Port Askaig. There I was greeted quite ceremoniously by the honorary secretary of the Islay Lifeboat, Neilly Macmillan. He entered my visit in the lifeboat logbook and induced Mrs Macmillan to treat me with tea and cake. After this he informed me that the coxswain could not be interviewed at Port Askaig because he was required to represent Port Askaig that evening at a darts competition at the White Hart Hotel in Port Ellen. At that moment the familiar countenance of Archie, the Port Askaig/Feolin ferryman, appeared in the door putting the strangely timely question, 'You wouldn't be wanting a taxi to Port Ellen right now, would you?' We arrived at Port Ellen's White Hart Hotel later that evening to be informed that Donnie the coxswain was so tired after the darts match that he had to be taken home to Port Askaig.

I resolved that, to avoid any repeat wanderings, my interview with Donnie the coxswain was to take place on the mainland on board the *Loch Nevis* on her arrival at West Loch Tarbert and at my convenience. Donnie was, of course, entitled to claim his travelling expenses as well as reimbursement of his lost wages. This applied to wages in his four major occupations, part-time lifeboat coxswain, part-time rope catcher at Port Askaig pier, part-time whisky distiller at Caol Ila and part-time assistant to his gamekeeper son at the Dunlossit Estate.

Later that November the *Isle of Gigha* was slipped at Scotts at Bowling and I could do a proper hull inspection. This confirmed the existence of multiple fractures of the shell, mostly radiating from the rudder bosses port and starboard and from the joints of the skegs to the shell. A circumferential fracture in a weld on the port side of the stern was so wide that one could look out through it and admire the landscape when in the after-peak compartment. The starboard rudder-stock was found fractured and the rudder, of course, was missing. The port rudder-stock locking weld to the palm was found cracked right around, which was bound to impair the ship's steering ability.

When the taking of depositions and the hull inspections were completed I made my Preliminary Inquiry Report to the Board of Trade headquarters, in which I listed four causes of the casualty. In ascending order they produced a cumulative angle of heel from which the vessel could not recover. These were:

1 Omission to secure vehicles which allowed them to move on the deck.

2 Omission to break the metal-to-metal contact between the

undercarriage wheels of the forward trailer and the steel deck, which probably contributed to the collapse of the undercarriage and facilitated the shift of cargo.

3 Slack water in the after-peak and the engine room.

4 Cracked rudder-stock detracting from the vessel's steering capability.

Having stated in my report the causes of the casualty as I saw them, I named the contractors, the managers and the master in their different ways as having been responsible for the disaster. I emphasised the circumstances as regards the blame attached to the master. He had been asked to operate an undermanned vessel in which he had to concern himself with engine room maintenance at the same time as with navigation and safety of cargo, and was under commercial pressure by the managers. I pleaded that his foreign-going master's certificate should not be interfered with as it was not required for the trade he was engaged in. I also made a strong plea for instituting a Court of Inquiry rather than prosecution under the Merchant Shipping Act, as it would be better at providing publicity for the hazards of this new means of transport and satisfy a considerable local interest on the West Coast of Scotland.

I did not receive a great deal of support for my recommendations at headquarters. I was made to understand that the incident had occurred hundreds of miles away, in a sparsely populated part of the country, and that it hadn't evoked much interest in the media. In view of this attitude 'up on high', I telephoned the editor of the *Campbeltown Courier* and dictated to him a front page leading article for his next issue. The following leader entitled 'WHY THIS INQUIRY IS NEEDED', in large letters, appeared on the front page of the *Campbeltown Courier* of 20 April 1967.

Before Scottish Secretary William Ross makes his all-important decision on future sea services to Gigha, Islay, Jura and Colonsay, there are one or two questions which need to be answered. The choice Mr Ross has to make is between a conventional MacBrayne's car-carrying steamer and an 'overland' route utilising short-haul ferries making several trips per day.

Five months ago, two men lost their lives when a flat-bottomed ferry taking lorries to Islay overturned in a moderate sea. Before the fare-paying public learns whether this type of vessel is going to be the only one in service, it is essential that we know how safe these vessels are. Accidents do not just happen. The word 'accident' indeed, is one to be avoided, since it implies an occurrence due entirely to chance. It can therefore be applied to very few incidents.

What are usually called accidents are nothing of the kind. They do not happen. They are caused. Something, or some things, made the ferry boat *Isle of Gigha* overturn on November 11th. Before Mr Ross makes his decision, the public must know what. Either there was something wrong with the boat in design or construction, or she was wrongly loaded or badly sailed, or the mishap was caused by some external factor or factors.

Either way, the public must know which explanation is correct. Idle speculation by non-experts is both profitless and wrong. The only body qualified to state the cause of the disaster will be a Board of Trade Inquiry. An inquiry can settle, once and for all, the question whether this type of vessel is safe for all-year-round use on the open sea with passengers and vehicles aboard. It can also draw attention to the particular precautions which need to be observed in operating such boats.

The public needs such reassurances. Until they are given, no-one can be really happy about the vessels to be employed on the 'overland' route. Until we know what made the *Isle of Gigha* capsize, there will remain a lot of understandable prejudice in favour of the good, old-fashioned heavyweight steamer.

That issue of the *Courier* was promptly sent to the Board of Trade London headquarters and, lo and behold, a formal inquiry was ordained! The Board of Trade was to be, as usual, represented by Duncan MacNiven WS, senior partner of the Glasgow solicitors, MacGrigor Donald. He duly received a phone call from Sheriff MacDiarmid of Argyll who suggested Campbeltown Sheriff Court for the inquiry. He thought it might be an interesting change from the usual succession of petty driving offences.

The Sheriff presiding over the court of inquiry was to be assisted by three assessors, a retired commodore captain of Cunard, a retired captain of P&O and Professor Conn of the Glasgow University Department of Naval Architecture. On the morning of the opening day I accompanied the assessors from Glasgow to Fairlie and then on board the *Duchess of Hamilton* to Campbeltown. I thought this would be the appropriate means of travelling on this occasion, an auspicious one for the marine industry.

In due course I was invited to deliver the case for the Crown as outlined in my preliminary report. Captain Pond, a nautical colleague, reinforced my case on the subject of undermanning. Duncan MacNiven was closely watching the Sheriff's face as I developed my case. As long as it looked awake and reasonably interested, he would signal to me to go on. When it began to nod off, Duncan's gesture would advise me to wind down. A good part of the proceedings was taken up with the cross-examination of witnesses by various lawyers, and primarily by Duncan MacNiven on the Crown's behalf. My job was to sit behind him and pass him questions scribbled on wee scraps of paper. On one or two occasions he turned to me and asked whether the question was going to do us any good or was it just going to embarrass the witness. I have learned much about simple decency from wise old Duncan.

The verdict of the Court leaned heavily against the master of the ship, Gordon Graham. While stopping short of recommending the suspension of his master's certificate, it censored him and blamed him entirely for the casualty because he didn't secure the vehicles. The managers of the Eilean Sea Services and the contractors escaped scot-free and were even commended for introducing the idea of a roll-on-roll-off craft on the West Coast of Scotland.

I wrote to the Board of Trade headquarters drawing their attention to the offences that had been committed under the Merchant Shipping Acts. For that reason alone, I said, there was a more than sufficient basis for instituting a re-hearing on the grounds of miscarriage of justice. There was also the need to publicise the various aspects of safety that came to light in the Crown's submission and had not been highlighted in the Court's verdict. In reply, I was told that the Treasury Solicitors advised against ordering a re-hearing as the expense involved did not justify the risk of the charge of 'miscarriage of justice' not being upheld.

The salvaged vessel was returned to the Eilean Sea Services of which Gavin Hamilton was chairman and major shareholder. He asked for my advice as he, a landscape gardener, was not sure what to do with the ship on his hands. Next time I was at Lithgow's shipyard I mentioned the *Isle of Gigha* to Sir William Lithgow. Not many weeks later Western Ferries Company was formed with the participation of Sir William, his cousin Ian Harrison of the Harrison Clyde Shipping Company, a few other directors of that company, and two or three Argyll shareholders. They bought the *Isle of Gigha*, re-named her *Sound of Gigha*, had her overhauled and fitted with buoyancy trunks on deck, port and starboard, which considerably increased her range of stability. She was temporarily put into casual service transporting commercial vehicles to the nearer Western Isles. When the somewhat larger ferry the *Sound of Islay* was built to Western Ferrie's account at Ferguson Brothers in Port Glasgow she was put on the regular service between Kennacraig and Islay and the *Sound of Gigha* took on the ferry service between Islay and Jura in which capacity she successfully performed for some thirty years.

5

MORE SHIPWRECKS

Lochiel, *1960*

It was the day of autumn cattle sales in Tarbert in 1960 and the *Lochiel* was making her way up West Loch Tarbert full of cattle and sheep. The weather was calm and the visibility good. About a mile from the pier she struck a rock and fetched up with her bows in the mud. The cattle sales had nothing to do with the cause of the accident, which was the direct result of the usual helmsman being away, singing at the Mod.

The *Lochiel* belonged to that more gracious age of MacBrayne ferries when you were served by white coated stewards in an Adam green dining saloon; where silver cutlery gave its own particular warning of imminent departure by vibrating noisily as the main engines were started. Several plus-foured members of the gentry were sipping tea in the comfort of the forward lounge when a rippling tremor ran through the ship; the engine room emergency escape route ran into the saloon and the sealed door

Postcard of *Lochiel* at West Loch Tarbert

burst open to reveal a dripping second engineer. 'My God we're sinking!' he shouted, and disappeared towards the bridge. After a few moments silence there was the sound of a cup being replaced onto its saucer. 'I suppose we should go and see to the dogs', someone said.

The little ship had run into Sgeir Mhein, an unmarked skerry submerged at high water, which normally merited a dogleg in the otherwise straight run up the loch. In absentmindedly steering by eye rather than by chart and compass, the vessel struck the rock a glancing blow with her port side, opening up a huge gash in the engine room. The master did his best to make for the pier, but as water rose over the main engine air intakes, she stopped and drifted into the mud just north-east of Eilean da Gallagain. There was no immediate danger since the vessel had sunk as far as she was going to and the main-deck was still above water. Passengers wandered around in bemused fashion as the crew frantically tried to disturb the lifeboats comfortably settled on their chocks since the last Board of Trade inspection. With a compassionate turn of mind, someone released seventy-five sheep from their pens and these relieved animals added to the surreal scene as they scampered around the decks.

The bar was in those days in the forepart of the vessel, the part which was disappearing under water. The valiant barman stuck to his post, with water nearly up to his armpits, salvaging the contents of the bar. He was handing out bottles of booze to all comers although the sea was lapping their waists, prompting one daily paper to headline the event: 'DRINKS FOR ALL AS THE SHIP GOES DOWN'.

The mess-room boy was left behind in the mess-room, having his tea. He decided that there was something wrong when he felt water round his feet. There was, alas, no orchestra to play 'Nearer my God, to Thee'; but perhaps a more appropriate tune would have been 'What shall we do with the drunken sailors?'

Bruce Howard, who lived on the loch side at that time, had a phone call from 'Big Alaistair' Cumming, MacBrayne's agent in Tarbert, asking if he could render assistance. He went to the scene in a 16-ft launch appropriately called *Bubble* and spent the night ferrying passengers and crew ashore and some salvage crews to the stricken vessel. One elderly seaman summed up the situation: 'Yon was a terrible experience altogether. I jumped into a lifeboat and there was no room for me, it was full of passengers and sheep.'

Within an hour, lifeboats rowed by some of the crew and some happy passengers ferried Tarbert fire-brigade men and pumps to the ship. The pumps were raised by ship's derrick and swung in through forward windows. In time the pumps achieved enough reduction in water level to allow the watertight door between the engine room and the shaft tunnel to be shut. The *Lochiel* was eventually salvaged by the salvage vessel from the ex-boom defence base in Greenock. The hull had to be freed of a vast quantity of mud. The master lost his job and fetched up as pier-master at Lochaline, not quite the West Highland equivalent to being exiled to Siberia.

I was not personally involved in the investigation of this casualty and the story is second hand, mostly as told by Bruce Howard. My involvement was with the renovation of the *Lochiel* at Lamont's yard in Greenock. I fell out with MacBrayne's engineer superintendent over trying to persuade him to encompass in the renovation specification, a toilet for the master's accommodation abaft the wheelhouse. He was still expected to negotiate two decks in search of a loo.

Rejuvenated by Lamont's, *Lochiel* chugged happily up and down West Loch Tarbert for many years, although always with a black line inside her engine room, which marked the high watermark on the day of the autumn sales at Tarbert.

Cessnock, *1968*

In January 1968 the 188-ft long bucket dredger *Cessnock* was working alongside Greenock's Princes Pier abreast a 202-ft hopper barge, slightly less beamy than the dredger and a good bit higher out of the water. On the evening of Friday 28 January the dredger was moored for the weekend alongside Princes Pier facing downstream with the hopper barge on the outside facing the same way.

The dredger was held by the permanent dredging anchor, two bow anchors and a stern anchor. The port quarter chain was secured to a quay bollard astern. There were 190 fathoms of chain in the main chain locker. The hopper barge was secured by bow and stern wire springs, three sisal forward-springs and two sisal after-springs. She was lashed to the dredger with bow and quarter sisal ropes. The barge was so much higher out of the water that the top of her belting was just about in line with the top of the dredger's forward fender post. All windlass brakes were off and none of the claws secured. On the night of Sunday 30 January the dredger had a lay-up crew of three men and the barge had two.

During Sunday night the southwesterly gale, blowing offshore at right angles to Princes Pier, was steadily soaring. Between 1.00 and 2.00 a.m. there were gusts of 75 knots. The gale and the surge caused by an abnormally high tide parted all the ropes and chains of both vessels, except for the rope lashing between the two bows and the dredger's main anchor chain. The two vessels started to drift, swinging on the dredger's main anchor chain, which remained taut as it was free to pay out under the force of the wind because the windlass brakes were off and the claws unsecured.

The dredger master's first reaction was to anchor her by lowering the bucket ladder, but after a weekend's lay-up there was not a sufficient head of steam to do this. He instructed the crew of the barge to let go her bow anchor pending steam pressure being raised and the bucket ladder lowered.

The two vessels were moving in a northeasterly direction while describing an arc of increasing radius, the centre of the arc being the main dredging anchor. The arc's initial radius was the distance between the anchor and the quay and the final radius the total available length of the chain. Somewhere along that arc the barge dropped her starboard anchor. About fifteen minutes after the two vessels broke loose, the bucket ladder was lowered. It seems reasonably certain that by that time the two ships were stationary, their position having been determined by the length of the dredger's main bow chain and the barge's starboard bow chain.

It seems also reasonably certain that due to the abnormally high tide, the ladder did not touch bottom when lowered. However the dredger's crew thought that the ladder touched bottom at high water and decided to raise it somewhat before low water at 7.00 a.m., to prevent it being pushed up with the falling tide and slackening the hoisting wires on the pulleys.

During the night the wind blew up to Force 12 and the bow lashing between the ships had to be replaced and re-secured by the crews. The ships were being buffeted against one another forward, and lying apart aft. The angle between them, of about 80°, was that between the dredger's and the barge's chains, leading north-west and south-west respectively.

Daylight broke at about 8.00 a.m. on Monday and the weather moderated, which allowed inspection of the damage inflicted on the dredger's starboard forward fender post by frequently bumping the higher riding barge's massive belting. The post was bent inboard tearing a sizeable hole in the deck. With seas surging between the ships, water was constantly washing over the starboard foredeck and pouring into the hoisting machinery space through the opening. The dredger's crew noticed water in that compartment only after it rose above the floor level. They flashed boilers and raised steam pressure from 100 to 120 pounds per square inch to commence pumping the common hoisting machinery and chain locker compartments.

During the morning the crew of the barge attempted to detach the barge from the dredger but the barge's anchor cable appeared to be fast. At about 9.20 a.m., with weather moderating, a tug came close to the dredger and the barge. The tug-master found the two vessels pointing to the flood tide and wind, the dredger having a slight list to starboard and the barge without a list. The two anchor cables appeared to him under heavy strain. He saw no one on deck and assumed that no assistance was needed.

At about 9.30 a.m., without any apparent warning, the dredger started to lean towards the barge and pulled her to port until the connecting bow rope parted. The barge then came upright and the dredger slid down her port-side and was upside down within seconds.

I put the story together up to this point using statements of various witnesses. There followed divers' examination of the upturned hull when bodies of the dredger's three crew members were found trapped by the port handrail. This gives an idea of how quickly the capsize had happened. When I went through the hull after salvage I discovered that:

1   There was no damage to the hull to account for the admission of water, apart from the tear in the foredeck starboard.

2   The hoisting engine barrel had 16 turns of topping wire out of a total of 26. This meant that the ladder was only about 40% down from its stowed position.

3   In the control room, the drain valve was seized in the 'shut' position, the gear lever seized in the 'hoist' position and the brake seized in the 'off' position. The steam valve was cracked 'open'.

Next came my job of investigating the casualty and trying to explain the puzzling circumstances listed below and to discover their cause:

1   The dredger heeled only very slightly and the barge had managed to remain upright to within seconds of capsizing.

2   The suddenness of the capsize in the absence of any external agency.

3   The ladder was discovered two-thirds up on recovery, whereas it had needed to be raised only fractionally at low water.

After some months of investigating and experimenting with another steam bucket dredger, I arrived at a hypothesis that seems to provide the most likely explanation. The chain of the barge's anchor dropped when

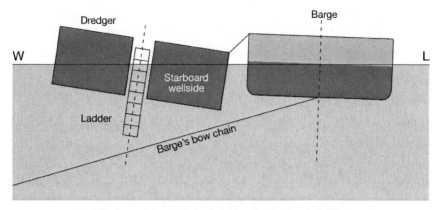

The barge's bow chain held by the dredger's ladder

drifting and was leading across the dredger's bow. The bucket ladder, when lowered, had swept that chain under the dredger's keel and held it there. The situation that arose is illustrated on the drawing above.

It is very likely that, after raising the ladder slightly, the dredger's crew, as was common practice, left the steam valve 'cracked', i.e. opened about one-sixth turn, the gear lever in 'hoist' and the brake in 'off' positions. Some time later the steam pressure was raised from 100 to 120 pounds per square inch to start bilge pumping. This caused pressure to build up behind the valve, making the engine start sporadically and winding about one turn of hoisting wire on the barrel at a time. This would have made the ladder creep up. The process went on until the ladder had crept up sufficiently to release the chain from under the dredger's keel. Presumably this would have been about two-thirds up.

The events that could then be expected to follow have been corroborated largely by the story as told:

1. The release of the barge's chain allowed the two ships to drift slightly downwind. The bows would however be checked by the dredger's chain and pulled towards Princes Pier. This would explain the observed heading into the wind.
2. Equilibrium between the two ships having been upset, the dredger started to go over by the bow due to the quantity of water in the starboard forward compartment. This would have pulled the barge down to port.
3. The two ships went on heeling towards each other but with the increasing heel, the barge's righting moment was rising, putting a breaking strain on the rope.

4 Following the breaking of the connecting rope, the barge came
   upright and the dredger continued to heel, water now freely
   entering the starboard forward compartment.

Flying Wizard, *1971*

The Dutch cargo-liner *Gaasterdyk* of some 500 feet length and six holds
was bound for the container terminal at Princes Pier, Greenock on the
morning of 8 November 1971. The pilot, Alexander McGugan arrived on
the bridge and put the engines on to dead slow, heading east. He asked
the bow tug *Vanguard* to make fast on the starboard bow and the stern
tug *Flying Wizard* on the starboard quarter lying up i.e. heading in the
same direction as the *Gaasterdyk*. The pilot then put the wheel hard to
port and the swing commenced, then he rang 'Dead Slow Astern' and
ordered 15° of starboard rudder to assist the swing.

The *Flying Wizard*, which had been running parallel to the *Gaasterdyk*
at half speed, moved out to the towing position on the starboard quarter.
She increased speed to full ahead with the strain on her towing wire and
her bridle fully out. The bridle was a wire that ran from a shackle on the
towing wire through a snatch block aft to a winch. When fully taken in,
it transferred the pivoting point from the tow hook to that after snatch
block. At this time the *Vanguard* was going round the *Gaasterdyk*'s bow
to take up her towing position at right angles to the port bow. In effect
the *Flying Wizard* was the first tug to exert the swinging force. The stern
of the *Gaasterdyk* came towards the *Flying Wizard* and appeared to gather
way, which placed the tug in the ideal girding position, heading up the
river and lying nearly abeam of the towed ship.

The pilot noticed the *Flying Wizard* listing over to port with her bulwark
in the water and tried to contact her on the VHF. On receiving no reply,
he stopped the engines and went out to the starboard wing of the bridge
and shouted to the *Wizard* to slip her tow. He warned the *Vanguard*
to prepare to let go and assist the *Wizard*. On board the *Flying Wizard*
the tug-master was in the wheelhouse with the mate at the wheel. One
deckhand was at the winch control and the other was trying to close the
port accommodation door, but as the vessel listed to port he placed only
one dog on the door. The first deckhand, on hearing that that the tug was
going over, left his position at the winch and joined other crew members
forward on the starboard side, as did the second deckhand.

Meanwhile on the *Wizard*'s bridge the tug-master was surprised by the

Gaasterdyk's stern coming up on him. He eased up on his engines and told the mate to put the wheel hard to starboard to slacken the tow wire and swing his tug stern to. He also gave two rings on the deck bell to tell the winch control deckhand to take in the bridle as the tow rope slackened. The tug righted herself and water was seen coming out of the deckhouse. The deckhand was not in his position, but standing forward.

As the tow restarted, the *Wizard* rolled over again to port with the towed ship's stern moving away from her, the ship heading roughly north. The tug-master then opened the port wheelhouse door and hooked it back. He told the mate to release the tow hook. The mate tried and failed to release it and the tug-master's attempt met with no more success. He went back into the wheelhouse, and as he did this water started to come into the wheelhouse through the open port door. The port accommodation door also flew open and water entered the cross-alleyway and poured down into the lower accommodation. On the bridge of the *Gaasterdyk* the pilot saw the position of the tug deteriorating and put the engines to 'Dead Slow Astern' to try and ease the weight on the tow wire and to give

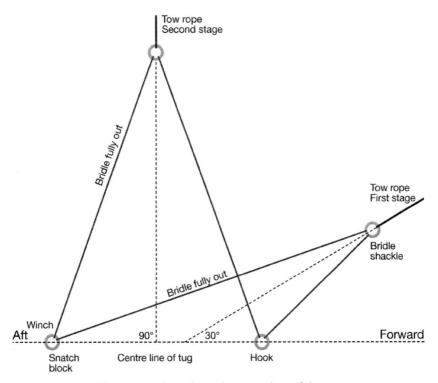

The tow rope's angle to the centre line of the tug

himself a chance to slip the eye of the tow wire off the bitts. This astern movement did not ease the strain and the engines were stopped to prevent the ship getting too much sternway on. The tow wire was then cut with an axe by an able seaman on the *Gaasterdyk*.

On the *Wizard* a deckhand tried to reach the hand release mechanism on the tow hook but slipped and had to be pulled back. The motor launch *Ranger*, ordered by Archie Munro of the Clyde Marine Motoring, tried to come alongside the *Flying Wizard* bow to stern, but as the tug was still going ahead, did not succeed and had to come alongside bow to bow. The tug-master was trapped inside the wheelhouse, water was rising up to his chest and the starboard door closed. However the mate heard him shouting, helped him to get out through the starboard door, down the hull and on to the *Ranger*, which had already taken on board the four other crew members. The *Flying Wizard* was lying on her port beam sinking bodily with the bow the last part of her to disappear.

The usual investigation of the accident followed and statements by witnesses have helped in writing the story. The investigation led my nautical colleague and me to this conclusion:

1 The primary cause of this casualty appeared to us to have been the failure of the crew to take in the bridle when it was possible, and so to transfer the pivoting point to the stern. This would have had the effect of the turning moment producing a movement of translation instead of one of rotation.

2 The secondary cause was thought to be the tug's reserve of stability being insufficient to resist not only an upsetting moment produced by a slow drag, but even one resulting from the effect of the tug's own propeller thrust on her rudder.

Subsidiary causes may have been the design of the tow-hook release mechanism which failed to operate at a large angle of heel and the crew's failure to secure the port accommodation door closed.

Loch Seaforth, *1973*

Loch Seaforth left Castlebay, Barra, bound for Tiree, in the wee sma' hours of 22 March 1973. The sea was rough and a swell was running caused by the Force 8 southwesterly wind. Captain Donald Gunn handed the watch to the second officer with instructions to call him prior to arrival in Scarinish, Tiree, i.e. after passing though the Gunna Sound.

Just before 6 a.m., with the Scarinish light on his starboard bow, the

The *Loch Seaforth* in East India Harbour, Greenock

second officer switched off the radar, which was making a noise while he was trying, without success, to contact the Scarinish pier-master on the VHF. After a while he sighted surf breaking over a rock on his starboard bow. He said 'We are too far in,' to the quartermaster and called for port helm. It was too late. The ship had struck Sgeir Uilleim skerry, shown on the Ordnance Survey map but not on the chart.

The master, now in the wheelhouse, tried to go astern and got the vessel stuck hard and fast on the rocks. In the engine room the chief engineer was trying to cope with rising water at the same time as a generator on fire. With the rising tide, the ship refloated and drifted, with the southwesterly wind and flood tide, north eastwards to a position off Port Ban.

Most passengers and crew were embarked into the first, (rowing) lifeboat. The third engineer was put in charge of the second, (motor) lifeboat, with the instruction to tow the rowing one. In the third lifeboat, the last to be launched, were the master and two directors of Caledonian MacBrayne. That lifeboat was met, and the VIPs in her helped ashore on Eilean Liath, by Hector MacPhail in his *Harbour Maid*; and from shore by Hector's wife Flora in her car. Hector and Flora also appear in chapter 3 of this book. The other two lifeboats were found and guided to Scarinish by the fishing boats *Saffron* and *Harbour Maid*.

The master and volunteers from among his crew returned to the *Loch Seaforth* shortly after 7 a.m. to await the arrival of the tug *Cruiser*. It was then that they found one cabin door locked, kicked it open and found a young man asleep in his bed. They gave him a cup of coffee and a life jacket. By midday of 22 March the *Cruiser*, with *Harbour Maid*'s assistance, brought the *Loch Seaforth* alongside Scarinish pier. At that time the water level in the engine room was 3 feet below the main deck and the same in the passenger cubicles forward of the engine room. The No. 1 hold was dry and No. 2 hold had some water in its after part. The lower accommodation aft and the shaft tunnel were not checked for lack of a torch. The checking and sounding was on the instruction of three CalMac superintendents who had arrived by air and, along with two directors, took over responsibility for the ship from the master.

There were no pumps available powerful enough to keep the ship afloat, pending the arrival of the salvage tug *Warrior*, expected next day. In the meantime, divers were attempting some plugging of the underwater shell openings and welding had commenced of the port cattle door. Discussions took place as to the possibility of beaching the ship, but this was turned down by the *Cruiser*'s master because his tug had too much draught for such an operation. The crew were passing their time lifting the mail and some of the cargo off the ship.

Early in the morning of 23 March the ship's stewards came on board to salvage the dining room silver and the contents of the bar. By the time the *Warrior* arrived it was too late for a salvage pumping. The ship had started to take water in quantity through the port cattle door, she then listed heavily to port till the foremast was resting on the pier, returned to vertical and listed to starboard before finally settling down some 30 feet off the face of the pier. The *Harbour Maid* was in attendance until the end.

Investigation of the foundering by my nautical colleague and myself, both before and after her salvage, and listening to witnesses, provided me with the story. The investigation led us to a conclusion as to the direct and indirect causes of the calamity. The direct causes could, according to my nautical colleague, be attributed to the officer on the bridge for:

1 Not following the course laid down in the pilot book and stipulated by the master.
2 Spending too much time trying to contact the pier-master on the VHF, instead of attending to navigation.
3 Not ascertaining his position by compass or radar, which he switched off.

The indirect causes of the casualty were, in my opinion:

4 Flooding of the compartments abaft and before the engine room, thus defeating the two compartments standard of subdivision of the ship.

5 The free surface effect of flooding, which destroyed the vessel's remaining reserve of stability.

The flooding of the passenger cubicles forward of the engine room could have been avoided if the ventilation trunks from the coffer-dam below, and passing through the passenger cubicles' space, had been welded properly after the previous grounding damage to the ship. The flooding of the compartments abaft the engine room could have been avoided if those spaces had been inspected and the leaking starboard shaft gland tightened up when the vessel lay alongside the pier on 22 March. The reason for not inspecting those spaces was given as not being able to get hold of an electric torch.

The vessel was salvaged and made ready for towage to a breakers' yard in May 1973. The crew of the huge German salvage ship that came to Tiree for that purpose did not appear to be in a pressing hurry, perhaps because they were made especially welcome on the island. When clearing customs on their departure from the south coast of England and asked for their destination they named the island of Tee Rae, which was taken to be a Pacific Island, and they were allowed a full consignment of duty free spirits. This may or may not have any connection with the welcome they received.

Glen Shiel, *1973*

The coaster *Glen Shiel*, which could be described as a second-generation Clyde puffer, was a steel motor-ship of 100 feet length and 9 feet draft, she had a 20-ft long forecastle and a 30-ft long poop. Three watertight bulkheads divided her hull into forepeak tank, cargo hold, engine room and after-peak tank. A thwartship wooden bulkhead divided the hold. The single 42-ft long cargo hatch was secured with wooden hatch covers and tarpaulins. The poop contained accommodation for the crew of five, engine casing and the steering gear compartment. The crew accommodation was lit by opening type side-scuttles. In the forecastle there was a store and a chain locker. A grab and a bucket were carried on deck.

On the evening of 28 June 1973 the ship was to load at Ayr a full cargo of coal destined for the Outer Islands and then to make way up the Clyde

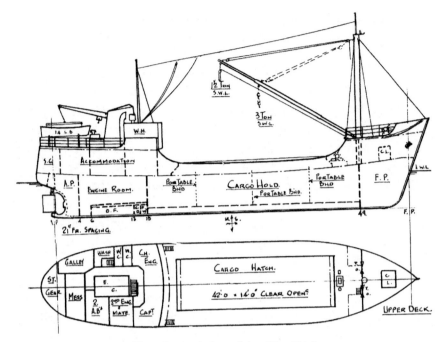

Elevation and plan of the *Glen Shiel*

to Shieldhall in Glasgow to pick up steel girders for the construction of the power station at Inverkip 'round the corner' from Gourock. The call at Inverkip was to be en route to the Islands.

Before loading the coal cargo about 5 tons of fuel oil was taken into the double bottom bunker. The after-peak tank used for freshwater cooling was not quite full and the same applied to the freshwater double bottom tank. The water ballast in the forepeak was being pumped out by the master during cargo loading but he stopped the pump to speak to someone and said that the tank was 'just about empty'. The shore electrician doing repairs in the engine room reported no unusual amount of bilge water there.

A full cargo of 215 tons of coal was loaded through the night, until half an hour after midnight, and was trimmed into the wings. The after half of the hold was well filled, except for a space under the bridge overhang; but in the forward half there were two wedge-shaped vacant spaces across the ship at the forward and after ends.

When loading finished all wooden hatch covers were put in place and the derrick housed on the starboard side. No tarpaulins were spread on the covers as the master was concerned that the steel girders to be loaded might damage the new tarpaulins. They were to be spread and battened down on the outward voyage from the Clyde.

The *Glen Shiel* sailed from Ayr at forty minutes after midnight with a complement of six on board, including one passenger. She was watched by the berthing master who saw her to be upright, to handle normally when clearing the harbour and to be two to three inches short of her marks. There was a Force 4 to 5 southwesterly wind at the time and a moderate sea. When the ship cleared the harbour the Master handed her over to the Mate and turned in and she motored at full speed on a northwesterly course with the wind and waves broad on her port beam.

So far, I have put the story together from various witness statements. The remainder of it I got from the sole survivor of the casualty, a deckhand, James Scott. After clearing Ayr harbour he was having his tea in the galley and the ship, although not rolling heavily, was taking spray through the galley portholes. It was clear to him that much more water must be coming over the bulwark and the hatch forward. In a little time it seemed to him that the ship was noticeably yawing, possibly needing large helm movements to stay on course.

Soon after James Scott had had his tea, he turned in and noticed the vessel rolling in a manner he hadn't experienced before. Two or three minutes later he was called by the mate who told him to get up on deck as *Glen Shiel* was taking a lot of water over the port side, some of it seeping into the hold, and developing a list to port. He didn't immediately heed the mate's warning, but a minute later he felt the ship give a lurch and he heard plates breaking in the galley. He went to the wheelhouse along the port alleyway in which there was some water, which meant that water was entering portholes on the port side. After the lurch the ship stayed at a steady list, which could mean that there was a shift of cargo.

When James reached the wheelhouse he saw water over the bulwark and one-third of the way over the hatch covers from port to starboard. He thought the list might have been 35° by this time. While the mate went forward to close the forecastle door the ship gave another lurch to port, which made three crew of the complement of six abandon ship. Then the vessel went right over, filled up and sank almost immediately.

In the course of the Preliminary Inquiry into this casualty which followed, my nautical colleague and I explored a number of possible causes that led this apparently well-found and adequately manned vessel to founder in moderate weather, shortly after leaving harbour and almost in the 'partially smooth waters' of the Firth of Clyde. The headings were:

1   The recurrence of flooding of the engine room.

2   Striking a submerged object.

3   Free surface in tanks other than containing oil fuel and fresh water.

4   Negligence in closing openings.

5   Defective stowage of cargo in hold.

6   Asymmetrically distributed deck cargo.

7   Inadvertent admission of water into the hold and engine room.

8   Admission of water into the superstructure.

9   Defective steering gear.

10 Inadequate reserve of stability.

Going over the headings, we had no difficulty in first of all eliminating two of the possible causes:

1   Although a recurrence of flooding had happened only four weeks earlier, when Troon Fire Brigade had to be summoned to pump out the engine room, the ship then traded for four weeks without apparent trouble. Also, had a large quantity of water again accumulated in the engine room, the electrician who had been working there on the evening of 28 June would have noticed it. Furthermore, the engineer would have been in the engine room after the pumping of the forepeak was stopped to change the valves. On the other hand, the apparent suspicion of four defective engine room valves causing the flooding, brings the ship's standard of engine room maintenance under criticism.

2   It is probable that James Scott would have known if the vessel had struck anything. We also discounted that possibility because the dock and that part of the Firth were regularly used by ships much larger than the *Glen Shiel* without incident. In addition, if this were to be regarded as an explanation, the list would have developed earlier than it did.

Coming now to some possible, if not critical, causes of the accident:

3   The after-peak tank being used for auxiliary engine cooling water created a virtually permanent free surface in that tank. The off-hand fashion in which pumping out of the forepeak tank was treated on the night of the casualty made one suspicious of slack water in that tank also. The unusual rolling of the ship noted by James Scott could be attributed to slack water in the forepeak. Slack water in those two tanks would have caused a noticeable reduction in the ship's reserve of stability.

5 With the ship's list increasing during the course of the fatal voyage there was a possibility of some coal cargo shifting to port into one or more of the void spaces. We thought it not unlikely that the lurch that made James Scott get up on deck was caused by a shift of coal of this kind. In preparation for giving expert evidence to the subsequent court of inquiry, I carried out experiments in my garden with a quantity of coal of identical quality and found consistently that an angle of 15° of heel was needed for the coal to shift. In reporting my experiment in their issue of 30 March 1974, the *Daily Mail* produced a headline 'D-I-Y Clue To Ship Tragedy'. A shift of coal would increase the angle of heel.

6 We could not be sure whether the slight list to port, due to the small quantity of coal and the grab and bucket being on the port side, with which the vessel arrived in Ayr, had been eliminated before departure We did not think, however, that such a slight list would have been critical.

8 It appears that in spite of a Force 4 to 5 beam wind on the night in question, some of the side scuttles in the side of the poop were left open. As a result, water found its way into the alleyway and the galley. What is more, James Scott saw the mate closing the sliding door in the forecastle bulkhead only when he came up to the wheelhouse shortly before abandoning ship; by that time 'water was pouring over the bulwark and reaching to about quarter of the width of the hatch on Port side'. It was not unreasonable therefore to speculate about the distinct possibility of enough water having got into the forecastle before that stage to produce a free surface. The effect of that free surface would be a small reduction in the ship's reserve of stability.

9 The ship had a history of 'sluggish' steering and although two rudder modifications apparently achieved some improvement, the vessel was still said to carry starboard helm, particularly in the loaded condition. It was also said that stern trim improved steering, maybe that was why the after-peak was permanently filled. Although there was no evidence that a steering defect contributed to the casualty, I could not help wondering whether an experienced master would not have avoided shipping beam seas had his steering allowed him to turn the ship's head into the wind.

Finally the causes which we thought to have been critical:

4 & 7 We thought that the most likely primary cause of this accident was the negligence in not battening down the cargo hatch with tarpaulins before proceeding to sea and the inadvertent admission of water into the hold in the prevailing conditions of full loading, sea and weather. It could be argued that the ship had in the past made similar voyages without battening down with tarpaulins, but this time the secondary cause played its part.

10 The secondary cause appeared to us to be the already moderate ship's reserve of stability reduced this time by slack water in the forepeak, in the hold and possibly in the forecastle. The reserve of stability became very moderate up to the critical angle of about 30°, beyond which the upper edge of the unprotected hatch coaming would become submerged and stability would rapidly disappear.

We stated in the Preliminary Inquiry report and repeated before the Court of Inquiry, at which I was in the witness box for two days, that these two were the principal reasons for the loss of the ship and the tragic loss of five out of the six men on board.

The Court of Inquiry held in the Glasgow Sheriff Court between 27 March and 2 April 1974 found that it was the absence of tarpaulins from her hatch that allowed the ship to take water into the hold and made her develop a list to port leading to a shift of cargo and the taking in of more water in such quantity as to cause her to fill up and sink.

6

SMALL CRAFT

Saxon

The *Saxon* was one of the longest surviving 'proper', i.e. coal-fired, steam puffers. Her 66 foot length was the maximum allowed by the locks of the Forth and Clyde Canal. She was built at John Hay's Kirkintilloch yard on that canal in 1903, under the name *Dane*, and sank in a collision some twenty years later.

The wreck was bought and restored to life as the *Saxon* by Finlay Kerr of Millport, owner of *Betty Kerr*, a 55-ft wooden Fifie yawl, boasting a boiler and a steam winch. Finlay's previous boat, the *Jessie Kerr*, a sailing ancestor of the puffer, was a 30-ton cargo smack with a fidded mast and long bowsprit. She had been built at Fife's of Fairlie. *Jessie Kerr* sailed into political history briefly at the 1910 election. Rosslyn Mitchell, trying to become an MP, was due to speak at Brodick but found himself stranded at Millport. Finlay and his *Jessie Kerr* saved the day. In the teeth of a 60 m.p.h. gale they made the passage, which the bewildered politician was to remember as the most momentous of his life.

While on the subject of politicians, the Kerrs of the island of Cumbrae are reputed to have been political refugees from the Isle of Arran, according to a legend that used to go around. It was said that their forebear, Iain Kerr Mor, or Big Iain, who lived in Upper Newton above Loch Ranza, took to 'stilling his own drams'. One day the exciseman appeared at his door in search of the still. Iain Mor lifted him gently, and gently dropped him into the loch below. After that emigration was inevitable.

Finlay's son, Walter, or Wattie, who inherited the *Saxon*, as a boy served his apprenticeship on the sailing smack *Jessie Kerr*. When he took over the *Saxon* she was driven by her original compound steam engine, which served her well till the end of her days, even if her haystack boiler had to be renewed. She was originally steered by a tiller on the after deck and it

Saxon at Millport with Wattie, Ernie and Robert

was only early in the last war that a wheelhouse, with a steering wheel, was put on her engine casing abaft the funnel.

Wattie and his *Saxon* became my steady 'customers' from the late 1950s on. When I thought that the *Saxon* was due for an annual load line survey, I'd stop at the number two Crinan Canal lock, and while engaging the lock-keeper in the usual chit-chat I'd drop the name of Wattie. 'Wattie' – the lock-keeper would chip in – 'Wattie's bunker is right in front of you' and he would point to a heap of coal. 'In such case, would you tell him, when you see him, that he is due for the "annual".' In due course I'd get a phone call from Mrs Kerr, 'Bring your weans along next weekend. I'll keep an eye on them on the beach and give them a piece when they're hungry. That'll give ye a chance to do the survey.'

Wattie had a crew of two on the *Saxon*, Robert the mate and Ernie the engineer who sometimes took his instructions from the number of stampings on the wheelhouse floor. This was only one of the many ways in which the *Saxon* crew did a bit of *Vital Spark* role acting. Their real

Saxon at a pier

opportunity in this respect came in the early 1960s. One fine summer day Wattie appeared at my door looking somewhat perplexed. 'Come in Wattie,' I said. Wattie came in and started scratching his head. 'Sit down Wattie,' I continued 'and have a wee dram.' Wattie scratched his head again and I suggested another dram to help him divulge his problem, *Saxon* was blessed with a BBC TV contract to be the *Vital Spark* in the *Para Handy* series. The next shooting was to be at Brodick pier on Arran and that happens to be outside the 'partially smooth waters' of the Firth of Clyde, beyond which a valid load line certificate is called for. The trouble was that Wattie forgot to ask me to do the annual survey when the time came for it and now the ship found herself at Brodick without a valid certificate. Would I oblige him by doing the survey on location at Brodick pier?

The part of Para Handy was on that occasion taken by Roddy McMillan whose face was to be seen in the wheelhouse window while Wattie, who was steering the boat in reality, was crouching below him. The sequence being shot was the one where the barrel of illicit whisky was discharged and placed on the pier awaiting the arrival of the police sergeant from

Lamlash. MacPhail, the engineer, was, of course, under the pier equipped with a drill and every kind of utensil he could lay his hands on. By the time the sergeant arrived, not only had the utensils been filled, but their contents tasted by the crew, with the result that the sergeant found all three of them horizontal in the after cabin. Para was just about able to raise his head sufficiently to inform the sergeant that they 'did not come under the Police but under the Board of Trade.' There was I, a living personification of the latter. It was too good an opportunity for the TV producer to miss. He tried to get me to appear in pinstriped trousers and bowler hat, to take a sip of the fluid in question and to pronounce, 'It is passed.'

In 1965 Wattie was about to sell the *Saxon* to a demolition company to be used in connection with the removal of a redundant Clyde bridge.

Saxon unloading at Corrie, Arran

I prevailed on Wattie to give her six months grace during which time I would try to find a museum prepared to pay £500 for the puffer and to preserve her. I went round the country in search of a safe berth for the *Saxon* but failed to find one. Had I been given somewhat more time, she might have become the *Auld Reekie* instead of the wartime-built fleet auxiliary tanker VIC 27, which was bought by Sir James Miller for the use of youth clubs.

My last memory of Wattie goes back to 1974 and that year's Clyde Week, based on Rothesay Bay. I twisted Wattie's arm to be the sailing-master on my *Lucy*, Dragon 25, in that week's races. He thrived on being under sail once again and was having the time of his life. He kept commanding us 'Give her all she'll take', and this meant taking quite a lot in a Force 5 to 6 southwesterly, when racing in the open Firth south of the islands of Bute and Cumbrae. The poor old lady has had to be bailed out ever since.

Wattie's brother Rab was skipper of the Largs to Millport passenger ferry in the 1950s and '60s. The ferry was the *Keppel* built for the 1938 Empire Exhibition in Glasgow, to take exhibition visitors a little way 'doon the wa'er' to see the *Queen Elizabeth* under construction. Years later I met Rab at the entrance to Edinburgh Castle, checking admission tickets in his retirement.

Wattie's friend the *Saxon*'s engineer Ernie Watt found a berth on the whisky puffer *Pibroch* after the *Saxon*'s retirement. She had just been fitted with a new Kelvin engine and Ernie kept her engine room in colourful apple pie order. It was painted white, the engine green and the brass and copper pipe-ork was regularly polished.

Alistair McKelvie of Brodick, Arran, tells of his first encounter with the *Saxon* about half a century ago, at the age of sixteen:

My uncles Finlay and Bobby Hamilton were regular emptiers of puffers. They were discharging the *Saxon* in Brodick with a cargo of coal, and were going to be pushed to finish her that day. At lunchtime they asked me if I would like to earn a pound by coming into the hold and shovelling for that afternoon. I jumped at the chance because you could buy a lot with a pound in those days. The coal was shovelled into big buckets that held a quarter of a ton, and then winched up on to the lorries on the pier. It was heavy, dusty and dangerous work. I worked as hard as I could and at four o'clock a big blister formed on my right hand and then burst covering the hand with water and blood and making the last part of the working day very painful. The men said I had done very well, far beyond their expectations. However they just gave me the pound! Once I had become a mature shoveller, two of us could do 120 tons in twelve hours and in those days three and sixpence a ton was good money. When you could get two cargoes in a week you would make about three times a tradesman's weekly wage. But I would not advise anyone to do it as a means of losing weight.

Alistair remembers puffer crews to have been, with a few exceptions, a wild lot of men. He thinks that the Para Handy crew one sees on television are like a band of angels compared to those he worked among. He recollects his best performance to have been in Lamlash when he, with Archie Hunter as partner, unloaded 135 tons of bagged Cumberland lime off 'Holy Willy' Macmillan's *Halcyon* in eight hours. The lime was in paper bags and when they got to the middle of the cargo the bags were hot, which made them very slippy and sore on the fingers. Willy Macmillan's *Halcyon* was a big, unusual boat, but a good one and well maintained. Willy was a very staunch adherent of the Free Church, hence his nickname of 'Holy Willy'. He would not tolerate bad language on his boat. Once, at Irvine, he promised the men discharging bricks off his boat an envelope if they unloaded in good time without swearing. In due course a bulky envelope was handed to the foreman whom the men followed to the nearest pub. There the envelope was opened and revealed a Wee Free tract.

'You Ken' Jock Henry was skipper on Hay's puffer the *Briton*. He was emphatic about all consumables being equally shared between himself and his crew of three. The crew were somewhat sceptical about the equality of sharing which used to be done by the skipper in his after cabin while the crew stayed in the fo'c'sle. One day the boy brought a large package for the skipper to share out in his cabin. The skipper duly divided up the dog biscuits out of that package but thereafter he became less emphatic on sharing.

The *Roman* was one of the finest boats in the trade. She carried 80 tons and could use a shallow berth. She was owned by a group of Arran people including the skipper Alistair Kelso from Corrie who kept her in superb condition but also worked her hard. He would discharge at Brodick, leave on the night tide, go to Troon, and get loaded under the big crane there, which was manned all night. Once loaded he sailed all night and would be at Lochranza the next morning and ready for an eight o'clock start. He did this regularly, calling at ports around Arran.

The customary crew's fringe benefit on coal-burning puffers was the surplus bunker coal left on deck. It was disposed of to replenish liquid supplies.

The author with the model of *Toward Lass*

A motor puffer that comes to mind is the *Toward Lass*, another of the wartime VICs that reverted to a puffer's traditional trade. She was normally looked after by one of the 'basic grade' surveyors in my Greenock office. On this occasion the colleague in question was on 'red alert' as his wife had just gone into hospital to produce for him their second offspring. He came to me with two options: either he would nurture his first offspring and I would 'do' the *Toward Lass*, or I could supervise his firstborn and he would 'do' the puffer. Having picked the first option as marginally the lesser of the two evils, I arranged for the *Lassie's* hull to be seen next day in Scott's wee dry-dock in Greenock. The condition of the *Lass* left a lot to be desired so I went over her like the proverbial dose of salts and in the process generated a hefty repair bill for Mr Burke, the owner. I fully expected an irate shipowner to come bursting into my office with the usual tirade against 'Big Brother'. Mr Burke did come and to my astonishment shook my hand and actually thanked me for having nearly demolished the hull of his vessel with my wee testing hammer. It transpired that he had just signed a fat contract with the US naval base in the Holy Loch and the ship had to be in first-class order. As a token of his appreciation he there and then presented me with a model of the *Toward Lass* which he had made himself and which I am holding in the photograph.

Bow and stern views of *Toward Lass*

When I arrived in Greenock in the late 1950s, Ross and Marshall's 'Light' puffer fleet was in its heyday. They were operating ten ships and the latest and most up-to-date of them was *Stormlight*, a smart coaster built at Northwich. It was still essentially a Marshall family business. Some ten years later Ross and Marshall joined forces with Hay Hamilton of Kirkintilloch, who owned a similar number of 'Cloy' and 'Nations' puffers. The combined fleet of Glenlight was sixteen ships, which until 1974 were still owned by the two participating companies and displayed their individual liveries. It was at some time towards the end of the 1960s that the newly formed Glenlight had to contend with the appearance of vehicle ferries, initiated by Western Ferries and taken up by the newly formed CalMac. The arrival of ferry-carried lorries on the narrow roads of the Western Isles spelled the demise of the Clyde puffer.

Caterina

Caterina was a twin-screw 75-ft long riveted steel cruising vessel built in 1924 by George Brown's yard in Greenock, for a gentleman of means, and registered in Glasgow. In the late 1950s she appeared in the Firth of Clyde, under the command of a rather shadowy and yet congenial mariner, undertaking cruises on the West Coast with an ill-defined number of passengers. Reports reached me that the seaworthiness and safety equipment of this mature vessel were not quite what might be desired. I sent a surveyor to Hunter's Quay in the Holy Loch, where *Caterina* was expected to disembark her passengers, but the skipper must have got wind of being pursued and chose Kilcreggan for his port of call on this occasion. When, at the end of following week we chased after *Caterina* to Kilcreggan, she landed her passengers at Largs.

In the end the crafty mariner must have sensed that the hot pursuit was getting too hot for him because he changed his port of registry from Glasgow to one in Ireland, obviously reckoning to be out of reach of the Irish surveyors. *Caterina's* enterprising skipper must have been disenchanted with Ireland when the intelligence reached him that our opposite numbers there asked the Greenock Board of Trade office to keep an eye on *Caterina* on their behalf.

At that stage *Caterina's* captain/owner started paying particular attention to a single lady passenger who was neither young nor old but rather well dressed and smart, in the way usually associated with Glasgow's professional women. She must have been enjoying cruising on the *Caterina* well enough to repeat the experience more than once. It seems that the relationship between her and the jaunty mariner came to fruition in the summer of 1960 when the lady found herself the proud owner of MV *Caterina*.

Somewhat overawed by suddenly becoming a shipowner she came to see me and we jointly decided that *Caterina* should spend a few days on dry land, preferably in James Lamont's ship-repair establishment in Port Glasgow. Once there, a small scaffolding was erected and attached to *Caterina's* side shell. When I attempted to climb the scaffolding to examine the shell plating, I became a bit disconcerted when a shell plate started coming away from the ship, with the scaffolding plank attached to it.

The poor lady spent her life's savings on having her ship repaired and equipped. She eventually presented *Caterina* to me, almost spick and span, new and complete with a seasoned skipper who was to take charge of her ship in the forthcoming cruising season. The young man was plausible and when I came to interview him at the same time as having a final check, I judged that he would go down well with the future lady passengers. The lifesaving and fire protection gear was all in place, but there was a slight hiccup over the navigation lights. They were pretty ancient and the lady shipowner was by that time getting a bit short of funds for buying up-to-date ones. The question was: would *Caterina's* side and masthead lamps produce lights visible at a distance of two miles, as called for by the Collision Regulations. I could think of only one way to answer that question and that was for *Caterina* to be in the Gareloch one night and heading for Garelochhead while I was watching her from the highest point of Whistlefield! The test needed pretty rigorous timing as there were no mobile phones for communication.

When I came across the *Caterina* towards the end of the summer season, I was not a little surprised to find that her 12-ft dinghy, the lifebuoys and even most of the fourteen life jackets had disappeared. The skipper and his crew told a haunting story of a freak wave, which washed the equipment overboard. And yet the good old bush telegraph conveyed tales of fishermen up and down the West Coast having been offered bargain priced second-hand lifesaving equipment and fire extinguishers. Contrary to generally held belief, a shipowner's life is not a bed of roses!

Roin Moir

Roin Mhor, (if the name was intended to mean 'A Big Seal' it should have been 'Ron Mor'), was a 47-ft wartime-built wooden twin-screw motor fishing boat. Her conversion to a cruiser was the labour of love of Jimmy Ritchie, a science teacher at the Inveraray secondary school. He was clearly also much dedicated to inspiring children with the phenomena of the universe because he constructed for them an ingenious working model of the planetary system.

Jimmy eventually gave up his teaching job to take up fulltime cruising on the West Coast with a handful of hardy passengers. He was a skilful, if somewhat ambitious, boat handler, handy with the boat's engines and well acquainted with the geography and navigational hazards of the Firth of Clyde and of Argyll.

Our relationship started on an amicable enough footing while I was telling him, as far as possible in common sense terms, of the relevant load line rules, which in simple language meant mostly plugging all the holes in the ship's hull and deck, and setting up sensible safety gear. In fact the little ship was already attended by a whole flotilla of small craft that could serve as lifesaving equipment, two six-person inflatable life-rafts, an 8-ft fibreglass dinghy, a 10-ft Red Rover inflated dinghy and a 12-ft Firefly sailing dinghy.

As time went on Jimmy began to see me as representing the Big Brother from somewhere in London, casting his shadow over all the wee boatmen

The 'wee bonny lassie' with the author's children and Jimmy Ritchie on board the *Roin Mhor*

on the West Coast of Scotland. Every request for the renewal of distress rockets or of a rubber gasket on a hand bilge pump met with a surly look and a threat of complaint to his MP about the heavy hand of Westminster-centred bureaucracy. In fact some highly charged missives went to the MP for Argyll and some of my time was taken up with answering questions thrown back at me by London headquarters. I don't know how the saga of the *Roin Mhor* would have been dealt with in terms of the cut and thrust of parliamentary questions and replies. I wouldn't have been surprised by a newspaper headline 'Roin Mhor – a ship scuppered by a bureaucrat'.

All that might have happened, were it not for a miraculous intervention of a wee bonny Scots lassie who came to share Jimmy's life afloat. She turned out to be not only an able first mate, but also one to be endowed with the precious quality of common sense.

Deli

Deli must have started life many years ago somewhere in the Mediterranean to acquire an appearance vaguely resembling a Spanish galleon. She was an ample-looking craft with two rather stumpy masts. She was brought to my attention by Mrs Kinneal of Ardpatrick on West Loch Tarbert. Mrs Kinneal was the somewhat uneasy mother of three young men who chose to lead a hippy existence on their mother's estate. What appeared to concern her in particular was their idea of making a paying concern out of *Deli* by taking passengers on cruises to sea out of West Loch Tarbert. She asked me to look over the vessel and give her sons guidance on how to make her seaworthy.

I spent a little time with the three romantically-minded gentlemen hippies, crawling over their boat afloat and talking them into plugging the obvious holes in the ship's deck and getting the basic safety gear on board. In the process I gathered that it would be ill-advised for this historic craft to venture far to sea without a pretty major overhaul.

My next step was to arrange a kind of a trial trip by chartering the boat with her crew of three for a wee 'hurl' from West Loch Tarbert to the island of Cara. I packed the deck with my three offspring and a friendly family with three more teenagers, all keen sailors. The day was fine with a moderate northwesterly breeze and the passengers offered to get the sails up. This was not a straightforward operation, even with the fore-and-aft rig. Halyards and sails were pretty heavy to operate, but they went up after nearly half an hour of concerted effort. At the passengers' prompting the engine was stopped and the portly vessel started making her way towards Gigha and her calf island Cara.

The wind was nearly following, but with short masts and a meagre sail area, the ship was wallowing in the slight swell, heaving, dipping and rolling to the mild discomfort of those on board. She was making headway in the Cara direction at a speed approaching 2 knots! I had the feeling that the romantic bubble was slowly bursting and with it the brave idea of cruises to sea!

Eilidh

Eilidh is a boat I well remember, partly because of her elegant lines and partly because she has had such a colourful history. It was in 1975, having been asked to survey her, that I made my acquaintance with this thoroughbred craft, then the property of John Mill.

Eilidh on a broad reach

An auxiliary cutter of 58-ft overall length, she was built in Dickie's boatyard in Bangor, North Wales, to the design of Alfred Mylne and to the order of Tom Russell (senior). The Russells paid £174 extra to have her teak planked. Perhaps that is why her hull was as good as new when I saw her forty-four years later. Tom called her *Eilidh*, Gaelic for Helen, which was the name of a much loved niece who died at the age of seventeen.

Tom and his family took *Eilidh* to the Baltic in 1936 and kept sailing her there for the next few years, at times racing with the Royal Norwegian Yacht Club. That gave Tom an opportunity to fall for the then new Dragon class and to have one built in Norway and shipped to Scotland. While *Eilidh* was based at Hanko in Oslo Fjord, Kaarlo, a young Finn came to inhabit her fo'c'sle as crew, cook and invaluable steward of the boat while the Russells were back home in Colintraive.

The German occupation of Norway in 1940 separated the Russells from their boat for the duration of the war. The Germans adopted her as a R and R (Rest and Recuperation) yacht for officers on temporary respite from the fighting fronts. *Eilidh* was well looked after during her 'war service' but the German officers never found the two bottles of pre-war whisky secreted under the gramophone. Towards the end of the war the boat fell into the hands of quislings who on the approach of Allied forces moved *Eilidh* from her moorings in the fjord to Oslo. They appeared to have holed her, probably in the hope of her sinking rather than being recovered by the Allies. Tom Russell and his family found her with the help of Karen, a Swedish girl, and in May 1947 they were going to sleep aboard her for the first time since August 1939. Just as they were finishing supper, Kaarlo appeared like a deus ex machina from the fo'c'sle galley in his steward's outfit, with a napkin over his arm, and asked 'Are you ready to be served coffee?'

Kaarlo remained with *Eilidh* and the Russells until the early 1970s. It was then that Tom's son Tommy Russell (junior), sixty at the time, reluctantly parted with *Eilidh*. With the family dispersed he found himself the sole owner and the boat too much of a handful for him. He sold her to John Mill.

In 1994 John Mill, in *Eilidh*, took a day and an hour off the previous Clyde to Brest race record and came first with the spinnaker torn and 'reefed', blowing her to victory. In 2002 she was sold to an enthusiastic owner in the South of France who restored her to her original condition with the help of a French Government grant.

Eilidh needed a crew of four. How lucky that Tom and Tommy Russell, John Mill and the Frenchman, each had been blessed with four children. I could not have told the *Eilidh* story without the help of Tommy Russell (junior), now 93, and his wife Shirley, a lady of much kindness and charm.

Six cargo boats and a gentleman skipper

This is a tale of six cargo boats and a Highland 'gentleman-skipper': a wee saga of one man's efforts to keep the puffer trade alive in the Islands and a little romance, adventure and misadventure mixed in with it. I gathered some of it calling on Hughie's fleet at times and some I derived from Josephine's scrapbook.

The skipper, Hugh Carmichael, was born on Lismore and came to Mull as a young boy when his father, Hugh senior, took on the Craignure ferry. Hughie went to the Lochdonhead school and it seems he was not always happy in it. With the outbreak of war he joined the Royal Navy and was on the destroyer *Encounter* when she was torpedoed and sunk in the Java Sea. There followed three and a half years in Japanese hands, building roads on Celebes. On his return home in 1946 Hughie was given a hero's

Hughie Carmichael

welcome with a ceilidh held in Lochdonhead school. Not that he thought of himself as a hero. When asked how long he had been adrift in the sea, he thought, as though counting, and said, 'Only about three days'.

Once back home at Craignure, Hughie took a hand in running the small passenger ferry from the then still pierless Craignure out to the Sound of Mull steamer *Lochinvar*. In 1950 he ventured into cargo carrying with the wee *Hilda* which could cope with a load of 12 tons, mainly of slate from Cullipool on Luing. With increasing trade, the 20-ton converted ring-netter *Monsoon* was added to the fleet. *Hilda* continued carrying general cargo while *Monsoon* was on the Skerryvore run, bringing in materials for rebuilding the lighthouse.

On my first encounter with Hugh, on board the *Monsoon*, I was struck by a glamorous pin-up on his bridge. While I was searching in my mind for the name of the film actress who could be attached to that pretty face in the picture, Hughie quietly told me that it was his wife Josephine. Later, out came the romantic story. One day in the early 1950s Hughie was loading hay on to *Hilda* at Oban pier. He was approached by two young

HMS *Encounter*

ladies and asked for a lift to Mull because they had missed the Mull ferry. Delphine and Josephine were ferried across to Grasspoint. They were actresses on their way to stay with the Leslies of Grasspoint, Delphine's parents. Josephine fell in love with the ferryman and they were married in 1953.

While on the subject of stars of the theatre, the *Monsoon* herself became something of a film star. She appeared in *Bridal Path* starring Bill Travers, and was involved in *Alive and Kicking* with Dame Sybil Thorndyke, and also *Touch of Larceny* with James Mason.

Shortly before Christmas 1960 the *Monsoon* was carrying lime from Fort William to Mull. Hugh had wee Donald 'Doicks' Macallister of Tobermory as his crew. They were approaching the north end of Lismore when the engine began to slow down with the flywheel throwing water all over the engine room. A little distance from Glensanda, on the Morvern shore, the engine died. They dropped anchor and while Donald fired distress rockets Hughie devised a raft from two oil drums and a plank. The two men, and a wee terrier, Hughie's constant shipboard companion, made their way through the icy waters of Loch Linnhe and then walked several miles before finding a haven in Mr Cameron's farmhouse at the head of Loch Choire. Next day, when Hugh returned to the spot where *Monsoon* was anchored, there was no sign of his ship, she had sunk without trace.

Dougals, a 66-ft seine-netter, was bought at Portavogie in Northern Ireland as a replacement for *Monsoon*. She could carry 60 tons and gave

Hughie and Josephine's wedding

Dougals

three years of faithful service, mainly carrying materials for the building of piers at Craignure and Coll. There were the odd hiccups, as when Hughie had to use brute force with an axe to clear *Dougals'* hold of solid tar. He was delivering tar chips for road-making at Inverie on Knoydart and they went solid on him.

Having been dutifully submitting *Dougals* to me for my annual survey of deck and safety equipment, Hughie could not face the trouble and

Bridge on *Shapinsay*

expense of the five-yearly load line survey, which called for the hull to be examined out of water. He temporarily gave up the cargo trade to try his luck at lobster fishing, made his creels the old way with hazel twigs and fish-boxes, while Josephine and the children made nets.

When the pulp mill opened at Corpach, Hugh saw the opportunity it offered, negotiated a loan and bought *Shapinsay* which had had a five-yearly load line survey and had a new certificate to prove it. *Shapinsay* started life as an Icelandic trawler of distinguished lines, was converted to a cargo vessel for Orkney-based Dennison Coasters, and then for Harry Banks of St Margaret Hope on Orkney was often used on the egg run from Orkney to Glasgow. She was 86 feet long, had a capacity of 120 tons, and was of sufficient size to carry timber from Mull to the Corpach pulp mill; moreover she had a large and comfortable skipper's cabin aft.

The Orkney boat attracted an Orkney engineer, Jimmie Hamilton, to join her. When demand grew Hugh bought *Marsa*, a 'gentleman's puffer' with which he continued to carry timber for a time, while Jimmy skippered *Shapinsay* carrying general cargo. Other crew members were Big Donald Maclean and wee Donald 'Doicks' Macallister. *Marsa* was a wartime VIC puffer, converted to a cruiser in the 1960s for our old friend Archie Kelly. She had a large and tall bridge-house, stretching across the width of the ship, with funnel abaft, unlike the original puffers. An auxiliary engine drove the winches, and there were advanced domestic facilities.

It was in the *Shapinsay* era that I found myself, with my young family, spending an Easter holiday at Lagganulva farm on Mull. The farmer's daughter, who was a cook, had just got married and left home for Torloisk,

Marsa

while the other daughter, a shepherdess by profession, had little culinary interest or inclination. We got cold mutton pie for breakfast, lunch and supper. It was therefore with great alacrity that we accepted Josephine's invitation to Easter Sunday lunch with the Carmichaels at Craignure.

Shapinsay had to be sold in 1967 to defray the loan taken to buy *Marsa*. She passed a load line survey to ensure her seaworthiness for the voyage out to St Vincent in the Windward Isles from where she was to trade. Hugh was asked to take her out and this he would have done had his friend and engineer Jimmie Hamilton been available, but Jimmie would have had to skipper *Marsa* while Hugh was away. A skipper and crew were hired by the new owner and set sail without delay and without getting to know the boat, and especially the peculiarities of her engine. While sheltering in a bay in southern Ireland *Shapinsay* dragged anchor, was blown on the rocks and wrecked. All her crew were saved, thanks to one crew member swimming ashore.

In 1972 a traditional type of puffer, the *Eldesa* joined *Marsa* in the timber trade, for most of the time. The one notable accident she suffered in nearly a decade under Hugh's command, which included an appearance in the film *The Eye of the Needle*, was when she damaged herself hitting the north pier at Oban. Hugh promptly contrived a cement box to stop flooding through the shell damage. He then proceeded with all speed through the Crinan Canal to Ardrishaig, heading for Lamont's repair yard at Port Glasgow. There was an anxious moment when the ship turned Ardlamont Point and got a bit of a battering from the southwesterly seas. Once out of the Kyles of Bute the skipper and his crew realised that they had not had time to provide themselves with a chart of the Clyde. They had to navigate up the river by the Esso road map and came in sight of the Erskine Bridge before it dawned on them that they had gone too far and had to turn back for Port Glasgow!

By 1980 when the pulp mill closed, trading with small vessels became an uphill struggle, largely due to the stiff competition from lorry-carrying ferries. In 1981, whenever cargoes were in short supply, Hugh and Mike, a gamekeeper of Torosay Estate and also a diver, worked at recovering coal dumped in the Sound of Mull by a Yugoslav ship during the war. Mike dived to locate the coal and Hugh and his son Shaun worked the winch and the grab. It was excellent Welsh coal and was shipped by *Eldesa* to Lochaline and to the Isles.

In 1983 Hugh sold *Eldesa* in order to retire. He delivered her to her new owner, Chris Nicholson, the laird of Easedale, into the tiny harbour of the island. She was to become a tourist attraction, to cruise round the islands and to dredge silt from the harbour, after an overhaul at Campbeltown shipyard. Hugh was relieved that his last puffer would be preserved and that he had found a good berth for her.

Hugh Carmichael was a wholehearted sailor who struggled bravely for the survival of a Highland enterprise; a struggle in which he would not have succeeded without his 'wonderful wife'. He was a modest and a mild man. One never heard him use a swear word, the nearest to it being his expletive 'by crickie'. He had two strong antipathies, the Japanese, and a woman teacher at Lochdonhead school who had been forever knocking the use of Gaelic out of him, as a child. I noted once the result of it when he responded in English to a Gaelic greeting by Mr MacCall the sea lock-keeper at Crinan Canal.

In 1981 Hugh was awarded a certificate of master of a home trade ship in recognition of his long and distinguished service as seaman and master.

Darthula II

Darthula II

The first Loch Etive boat I came across was *Darthula II*. I have been told that the name is Gaelic for Deirdre. She was the last boat built by Dickie's of Tarbert before the Second World War. A 60-ft long wood motorboat, she was delivered to Sandy Black, a cattle merchant of Taynuilt. During the war she was on convoy duties off the coast of Argyll and another mail boat took her place on Loch Etive. I have been told that in the winter of 1945 the loch froze for nine miles from its head and the Glen Etive people were without rations for weeks. In the end they set out with pack horses over the ice to meet the mail boat, which carried their supplies.

After the war *Darthula II* returned to Sandy Black's Loch Etive service. She carried passengers, mail and supplies to Glen Etive pier at the head of Loch Etive, starting from Taynuilt pier and calling at Inverliever and other jetties on the south and north sides of the loch. In the summer, the daily sailings to Loch Etive Head started at Achnacloich pier, to the west of Taynuilt, to which there was a rail link from Oban and which was part of a circular tour. Passengers were taken by bus from Loch Etive Head up Glen Etive and Glen Coe to Ballachulish station, from which there was a rail connection to Oban. The cost of the circular, all-day excursion was seventeen shillings first class and fifteen shillings second class in 1959.

Sandy Black inherited from the previous Loch Etive mail boat operator, a deckhand who was known as 'Captain Burns'. The 'Captain' wore a uniform with enough gold braid on his arms and cap to qualify as an admiral. Although far from young, he was very nimble and used to leap into a dinghy at various stops along the loch side and row to the jetties with the mail.

Some time in the 1950s Jack Lynn of Dalmally bought *Darthula II* and operated her until 1967. In that year Beeching's Axe put an end to the Oban to Achnacloich and Oban to Ballachulish rail connections and so also to the circular tours

Donald Kennedy, affectionately known as the 'Dooker' took over the mail, passengers and supplies run from Taynuilt to Glen Etive pier in 1967. His *Jessie Ellen* was a 45-ft wood motor boat of carvel, larch on oak, construction, built by Weatherheads of Cockenzie. In the mid 1980s the mail contract came to end but the 'Dooker' and later his son Donald 'Dooker' junior carried on. At the time of writing 'Dooker' junior runs popular pleasure cruises on the loch and does occasional deliveries of mail, passengers and supplies to Glen Etive on *Ann of Etive* a 66-ft long steel motor vessel built on the Thames.

In the early 1960s another cruising boat appeared on Loch Etive. *Etive Shearwater* was a 70-ft German gunboat war prize of wooden, double diagonal construction, owned jointly by an ex-Oban Provost and an ex-Oban solicitor. Based on Achnacloich pier, she was ably skippered by Boyd Keen, a colourful local character. Somewhat wild, pirate-like in appearance, Boyd could spin fabulous yarns, more or less historically accurate. Sailing past mountains that harboured golden eagles, Bonawe granite quarries and the Ardchattan Priory connected with William Wallace and Robert the Bruce gave a lot of scope for his tales.

My last survey of the *Etive Shearwater* was at Greenock in 1968, when after the Achnacloich pier was damaged in a storm, the boat was being prepared for a voyage to Ullapool. She was later working out of Arisaig.

The St Kilda Express

Since the last war there have been a number of attempts at running the 'St Kilda Express'. Two well-known boat skippers, one from Mull and the other from Mallaig, each tried for a while, more or less successfully,

Charna and St Kilda

to provide a service to St Kilda. Another skipper who tried it was little known until he gained publicity by stranding his passengers, not without provisions(!), on an uninhabited Monach island off the west coast of North Uist. He apparently had a bit of trouble with the boat, and as soon as that had been seen to he had to attend court for drunken driving. Meanwhile the 'toorists' sampled a few days of Robinson Crusoe existence.

Bruce Howard, then of Rhu Estate on the south shore of West Loch Tarbert was in 1968 able to realise his ambition of operating cruises around the Hebrides when he bought the 55-ft motor fishing vessel *Charna*. She was built as a ring-netter in 1955 but was later converted to leisure use by the addition of a handsome teak wheelhouse, a deck cabin and a new Gardner engine. Bruce had Timbacraft at Shandon to install in her two more double cabins and another WC and basin. He was then approached by the National Trust for Scotland, the owners of the St Kilda group of islands, with a proposal to operate with fortnightly working party holidays in summer, taking them to the main island of Hirta.

Bruce seized on this source of employment for his boat with enthusiasm and contracted to operate from Oban to St Kilda between early June and the middle of August. It was no small undertaking to make regular voyages of 125 miles of which the last 40 were to be beyond the doubtful shelter of the Outer Hebrides, out into the Atlantic in fact, with no secure harbour when one arrives there

It was the time when the Board of Trade suddenly woke up to enterprising 'plying for hire and reward' boat skippers making exposed passages off the west coast of Scotland with up to twelve passengers. What wakened the Board was the *Quesada* fatal accident. (The magic number of twelve is significant because a passenger certificate is needed when carrying more than twelve.) That would probably explain why the National Trust for Scotland said to Bruce that there was a requirement for the vessel to be examined by the Board of Trade, 'a mere formality'. That 'mere formality' was where I came in to break to Bruce gently the news that *Charna* needed a load line exemption certificate since her summer itinerary was hardly a 'trip round the bay' exercise.

Until that time I knew Bruce Howard only distantly through phoning him for a (paid) permission to pitch a tent, on a designated patch of his land, in which my wife and offspring could enjoy partial protection from the midges while I attended to pressing 'boat business' in the Tarbert Hotel. When, one day I came on board *Charna* in Tarbert harbour to start the Load Line Exemption survey, there was a somewhat scruffy looking painter working on board. I saw no point in talking to the painter on what I was doing so we both stuck to our own business till lunch break. Then it seemed natural to get pally and offer each other bits of picnic. In the course of this chumminess I introduced myself to the painter and he told me that his name was Howard. As I wondered aloud at the coincidence of his having the same name as the local laird, Bruce had to admit to being the boat's skipper/owner.

Bruce was naturally apprehensive about the load line rule requirements calling for 36-inch hatch coamings, etc., but with a bit of common sense on both sides we arrived at a working compromise that enabled *Charna* to face the hazards of the open Atlantic with the Plimsoll line engraved on her sides.

Thus it was that in 1969 *Charna* embarked on her first round voyage, a journey that she made well over 200 times in the next nine years, a world record of its kind. In between St Kilda runs *Charna* did long cruises amongst the variable Hebridean seascapes. Bruce was also able to take in her a party from the then Inner London Education Authority to the Sogne Fjord in Norway, where they studied glaciology. But it was the St Kilda run that was the greatest challenge; it took a strong heart and a stout vessel to face the grey Atlantic each Monday morning when *Charna* emerged from the comparative shelter of the Sound of Harris and started to lift to the white-streaked walls of water.

Bruce and I became good enough friends for him to tell me one day that in the long night watches he felt glad to have done, at the Board of

Trade's asking, all he could to be prepared for any disaster. Fortunately disaster never struck him and the only time in nine years *Charna* faltered with an engine breakdown, his relief skipper Patrick Banks, whom we met as manager of Dickie's boatyard, was in charge and he coped admirably.

There was one item of *Charna*'s safety equipment with which I made particular acquaintance and that was her inflatable life-raft. On one occasion a new (second-hand) vehicular ferry had been towed across the North Sea for the Western Ferries Firth of Clyde service. I was asked to inspect the vessel halfway along the Caledonian Canal with a view to allowing her to proceed under her own steam from there to the Clyde. A Western Ferries' engineer superintendent took me round the ship and asked me to wait a little for the inflatable life-raft, borrowed for the few days of the voyage round the Mull of Kintyre, to arrive. The life-raft was duly delivered in a wee white van and I helped to put it in position and secure the hydrostatic release before letting the ship commence her voyage.

Next day, after breakfast in the Tarbert Hotel, I came out to meet *Charna* in Tarbert harbour for her annual load line exemption and safety equipment inspection. I arrived just in time to meet a familiar wee white van returning *Charna*'s inflatable life-raft to her usual abode. Somehow one engineer superintendent succeeded in slightly reducing my faith in human nature and in making his employers wait patiently for a finite length of time before enjoying the use of their new (second-hand) ferry in the Clyde.

Tony Dalton, an ex-naval officer and an experienced navigator, now sadly incapacitated and yet bravely active as an author and in other ways, took over the St Kilda run from Bruce Howard in 1978. His craft was the *Pentland Wave*, a sumptuously converted 67-ft long fishing boat. She had an eight cylinder Gardner engine, to which Tony loved to listen, and a crew of Cubby and Kate Mackinnon of Kilmelford. But I am going to let Tony tell his own tale of his *Pentland Wave*, starting with planting the Union Jack on Rockall for the BBC *Nationwide* programme!

> We were lying stern-to the beach at Oban North Pier, trying to draw the prop shaft as the stern bearing had run and also damaged the shaft. A chap hailed me from the pier, and he turned out to be the producer, Keith. 'Can you take me to Rockall?' he asked. 'Yes,' was my reply. 'When?' 'How about next week?' 'Fine.'
>
> We exchanged numbers to settle details – and the charter fee – and then the panic set in. I had accepted a charter at short notice for a boat with a knackered stern bearing and duff prop shaft. But I badly needed the fee so

Pentland Wave at Rockall

we loaded the prop shaft and bearing into the Landrover and drove very early next day to a workshop at Buckie. In a single day they straightened the shaft and re-metalled the bearing, and, back at Oban, we were able to fit both during the next low water.

We sailed the next week, leaving Georgina and our two-week-old daughter rather forlornly on the pier! Up the Sound of Mull as the sun set; north of Coll, south of Barra, past St Kilda and on into the west. I was navigating by sextant and dead reckoning, and Rockall came up bang on the bow – very gratifying! Although it appeared flat calm there was an oily swell surging twenty feet up and down the rock, making landing perilous. Keith tried first and missed his footing and, as he said later, 'Inspected the seaweed on Rockall for far too long a time'. Cubby Mackinnon was an excellent seaman, and also a diver, and he had sensibly donned his dry suit for safety. He tried next, and timing the swell perfectly was able to step across from the dinghy to a tiny ledge, and from thence to the summit, where he erected a small flagpole and a large Union Jack. The weather showed signs of breaking, so we spent only a few hours on Rockall before St Kilda and home to Oban.

We took over the St Kilda run from Bruce Howard a year later. Normally we sailed about 1600 on a Saturday, transiting the buoy-lit Sound of Harris at night and arriving at Village Bay, St Kilda in the early forenoon. The Army invariably shuttled new and old work parties ashore, which was a great help, but gave us very little time to explore St Kilda. We sailed after lunch, arriving back at Oban early Monday morning – then two weeks later we repeated the exercise. St Kilda was always a favourite destination, although we were at pains not to guarantee a landing.

In 1979 Bruce bought the *Pentland Wave* and we bought a half share in the seventy-one feet long *St Just* and we continued the St Kilda run with her until 1982 – when the money ran out! One abiding memory is of an eighty-year-old lady passenger, who insisted in very rough weather on staying on deck, kneeling and holding on to the bulwark like grim death as St Kilda appeared on the horizon. 'All my life I have dreamed of visiting St Kilda.' she explained. 'At my age I know I won't do it again so I want to live every minute.' She died the next year.

7

MacBRAYNE AND THE CALE

'You wouldn't be wanting to stand the Captain a refreshment when he comes down from the bridge?' would be 'Black' Bob's greeting when I got on board the old *Lochiel*, homebound, at the last port of call, the Gigha pier. Whether you were working with MacBrayne's, or were simply a passenger, you soon became part of the fraternity, in fact 'a friend'. 'Chust you come into the steward's cabin, it's simpler that way'. In due course Bob the chief cook would disappear and reappear with a bottle under each arm. Down in the dining room, Hugh the chief steward was not only your culinary consultant but almost a catering instructor inasmuch as he would instruct you on what you were going to have to eat.

The oldest in the MacBrayne fleet in my 'care' was the RMS *King George V*, built in 1926, of the second generation of turbine steamers and boasting, at one time, high-pressure boilers and geared propulsion, which was quite advanced for her age. My annual inspection of her in East India Dock in Greenock would commence with going down into the boiler room. I would be greeted by Neilly Hardy, the second engineer, 'Just you go easy down there with your hammer. Don't break up our house and home!' House and home the ship truly was, spending ten weeks of the year in service from Oban, round Mull, to Iona, and forty weeks laid up in Greenock harbour. All the time the master and chief engineer were receiving 'speed allowance' because the ship was capable of steaming in excess of 18 knots.

Going through the ship's boiler room always required a preparatory diet. Whoever converted the old coal bunkers into oil fuel tanks didn't think of the poor surveyor having to squeeze his way between the back of the tanks and the ship's side frames he was inspecting. Neilly was a short and slim man and used to pave my way under the boilers like a snake. When I got stuck he would pull me through and mutter something about 'those surveyors living on the fat of the land'. The chief engineer was Archie MacVicar, a kind and convivial gentleman of Ardrishaig. He

King George V at Oban

was in the habit of thinking up hypothetical problems for the engine department which Neilly usually managed to solve.

When I inspected *King George V* in Elderslie dry-dock for the last time, she was forty-six years old. The ship's shell, which had not been very thick to start with, was being scaled with pneumatic tools to remove rust, before its thickness could be gauged. I would darken each scaled compartment in turn, to see if there was any daylight showing through the shell. When the ship had to come out of the dry-dock in a hurry, I had to stop the scalers. It would have been too risky to continue. All I could do, in the circumstances, was to seek out what appeared to be corrosion 'dips' in the remaining internal shell surfaces and fill them with 'plastic metal'. The knowledge of this, if broadcast, would not inspire the ship's passengers with confidence when going round Mull in a choppy sea!

Neilly, who in time took over from Archie as chief engineer, threatened that it would break his heart if *KGV* was withdrawn from service and his 'house and home' broken up. I bet him a bottle of 'Laphroaig' that she would celebrate her half-century in harness. Sadly, 1974, which would have been her forty-ninth year, was marred by two events: the ship's retirement to become a stationary canteen vessel for Bailey's the ship repairers of

Lochnevis at Colonsay

Cardiff and Neilly's heart responding, as threatened. Neilly had a heart attack and the only consolation was that my payment of that wee debt of honour put a smile on his face. Never was a bottle of malt used in a better cause!

One could rarely travel undetected on MacBrayne's ships. I was keeping myself to myself on board the *Lochnevis*, which was deputising for the regular *Lochfyne* on the Gourock–East Loch Tarbert route. Sitting at the little bureau by the lower saloon, I was quietly writing my reports. 'Would you be the Board of Trade gentleman?' asked a Jura-sounding passenger. When I owned up to it, he added, 'Mr Bobbie Templeton wants to know if you would do him the honour of joining him at the ship's bar?' We reached East Loch Tarbert pier where there was a MacBrayne's bus ready to take us the mile across to West Loch Tarbert where the *Lochiel* was waiting to take travellers to Gigha, Jura, Islay or Colonsay. Charlie Maclean of Jura, for such was Mr Templeton's messenger, asked if I would join them in the car Mr Templeton had hired for the one mile crossing. Halfway across the driver was told to pull up and Charlie disappeared into the depths of Tarbert Hotel. He reappeared with an oblong bulge under his jacket. 'Mr Templeton thought that we had better have reinforcements in case the bar on the *Lochiel* runs dry.'

When we arrived at the pier of Craighouse, Jura, Charlie Maclean, who was the island's postmaster, postman and taxi driver, took up his daily

Claymore approaching Tiree pier

job of delivering mail up and down the island. I was met by a car from Ardlussa, in the North of Jura, where I had a boat to survey. 'It's a pity you had to bother yourself,' I told the driver, 'Charlie here could have delivered me on his postman's round'. Everyone laughed at that. At nine o'clock that night, as I finished with the boat and we were about to sit down to supper, Charlie arrived with the mail!

Surveys of MacBrayne's fleet sometimes involved sailing with the ship, if it avoided delaying her in harbour. On one such occasion I was on board the *Claymore* out of Oban and bound for Tiree, Coll, Barra and Lochboisdale. In those days there was no separate service to Tiree and Coll, and the round trip involved overnight sailing. All the passenger cabins were taken up and I was allocated the wee spare cabin that passed for the ship's hospital. In my bunk, dead to the world, when lying alongside the Coll pier, I was wakened by a loud knocking on my door. An instruction came to evacuate the hospital and vacate my bed for a young mother in advanced state of pregnancy, bound for the Castlebay, Barra, Cottage Hospital. I regained the bunk, still comfortably warm, as we were leaving Castlebay harbour.

There were few navigation buoys and lights amongst the rocks of the West Coast in my days and MacBrayne's skippers did more pilotage work in a day than most of the deep sea masters do in a year. In all weathers and all visibilities they somehow 'smelled' their way from pier to pier with

The *Arran* in Oban Bay

amazingly few groundings. The *Lochiel* was heading for the Gigha pier on a dirty winter's night, with Captain Dan Macleod in command. Dan was a heavily built, slow off the mark man, just about ready to retire. We were amongst the rocks, within about 200 yards of the pier, when the lubricating oil pump on the port engine packed up. An Olympic sprinter could not have moved faster to the bridge wing than did Captain Macleod. He worked the engine room telegraph as he shouted instructions to let the anchor go, all in a matter of seconds, and another stranding was avoided.

There was no medal for Dan Macleod's action, nor was there one for Captain Sandy Ferguson when he brought the *Arran* round the Mull of Kintyre into the Clyde after she lost one rudder and the use of her steering motor. And nor was there one for Captain George Smith who steered her back to West Loch Tarbert, trimming by the bow, and braving a Force 10 southwesterly. *Arran* was the first of MacBrayne's vehicular ferries on the Islay run, converted from a Clyde passenger motor-ship to meet the competition of Western Ferries' low-cost and reduced crew *Sound of Islay*, followed by the *Sound of Jura*. The *Arran*'s trim calculation was based on the assumption that she would always carry some lorries. With no lorries, the ship was trimming by the bow, her rudders made vulnerable by being half out of the water and steering not very effective.

One might have thought that the designers of the *Arran*'s conversion would be mindful of the steering problems of the three purpose-built

Columba en route to Iona

vehicular ferries commissioned by MacBrayne from Hall Russell of Aberdeen earlier in the 1960s. The first of them was *Columba*, later reincarnated as the high-class West Coast cruise ship *Hebridean Princess*. I happened to be on board when Captain Colin Macdonald took command on the day of her maiden voyage, with young Robert Campbell, future marine superintendent, as mate. They were not enamoured with their new ship when they discovered that she had two screws but only one rudder, an arrangement that wasn't always going to help them to steer themselves out of trouble.

Loch Arkaig, a wartime wooden minesweeper, acquired by MacBrayne in 1959, was given an aluminium superstructure and was made to serve for twenty years on the exposed Small Isles run from Mallaig to Rhum, Canna, Eigg and Muck. MacBrayne must have used some mighty persuasive arguments to convince the Board of Trade headquarters that this wooden vessel deserved a Class II passenger certificate, in contradiction of the Passenger Ship Regulations. Perhaps wooden hulls, hurriedly built during the war were not intended to give as long and as stalwart service as *Loch Arkaig* did. Maybe that was why *Loch Arkaig* needed almost round the clock maintenance. Sometimes it was a major undertaking, such as the replacement of much of the sternpost, but most of the time it meant the never-ending task of keeping dry the accommodation spaces below deck. The ship carried every kind of supply for the Small Isles as deck cargo:

Loch Arkaig arriving at Armadale

drums of petrol, live animals, odd pieces of machinery, crates of furniture. It was not surprising that the wooden deck responded to such rough treatment by leaking in ever different places! *Loch Arkaig* ended her days sinking in the Mediterranean.

The 'ugly twins' *Lochmor* and *Lochearn* were built for MacBrayne by Ardrossan Shipyard in 1930. They had straight stems, 'chunky' cruiser sterns and insufficiently raked masts and funnel. What made things worse than the somewhat ungainly appearance was that, on launching, they were found to be grossly overweight. It was so much so that to enable them to carry the minimum weight of passengers and cargo, the steel superstructure had to be replaced by a light alloy one.

When I came to survey the 'twins' in 1957 I found that they had been allowed additional inches of draught 'for the duration' to enable them to perform their wartime duties. Since the 'duration' could be assumed to be over by 1957, the lost inches of freeboard had to be restored and that meant that the ships could just about carry their bunkers but virtually no cargo or passengers. The vessels' original designer, Professor Robb, was engaged to devise means of re-subdividing them so as to allow a deeper draught and the carriage of a commercially viable weight of passengers and cargo.

There followed a number of meetings with the professor in which words such as 'factor of subdivision' and 'permeability numeral' cropped up. I

Lochearn off the Isle of Skye

noticed that the MacBrayne's engineer superintendent was constantly taking notes. When I asked what he was writing he told me that though he was not well versed in the arcana of naval architecture, when reporting to his managing director, it might be useful to drop phrases such as the 'factor of subdivision' or 'permeability numeral'. In the end it was decided that re-subdividing the ship amounted to the erection of a new bulkhead across the engine room thus separating the main engines from the auxiliary generators. The work was done at the Lamont's repair yard in Greenock.

On the appointed day in the summer of 1958, I turned up in Gourock to attend the sea trials of the first of the re-subdivided ships, the *Lochmor*, Captain 'Squeaky' Robertson in command. In the course of conversation it transpired that the ship would, after sea trials, carry on to her station at Kyle of Lochalsh from where she was to resume the Kyle–Mallaig–Outer Isles service. I was a bit concerned about my wife coming to pick me up after the trial and finding me gone, but the problem was solved when my wife and our 1934 Morris Minor were invited to join me on the extended trial trip. We didn't allow the hitherto unknown sight of the undercarriage of our car while being lifted by derrick to spoil the occasion.

It was the time of the Queen's 1958 Tour of the Western Isles. The weather was truly royal and so was our progress up the West Coast. The sun was setting behind the Paps as we sailed up the Sound of Jura and

The *Lochfyne*

rose for us from behind the mountains of Morvern. We were berthed in the splendour of one of the staterooms in the port and starboard wings. My wife took a particular liking to the brass angled light fittings attached to the cabin bulkhead. To my relief I found later that I could avoid perpetrating unlawful acquisition of MacBrayne property by buying 1930 fittings in 1958 from a Glasgow ships' chandler.

There are, apart from *King George V*, at least two ships of the pre-war MacBrayne fleet that I hold in special affection. The *Lochfyne*, built by Denny's in 1931, had the distinction of being the first 'diesel electric' British passenger vessel, i.e. she had propellers driven by directly coupled electric motors powered by diesel generators. She was an elegant ship in the style of her day, with a cruiser stern and two funnels, one of them a dummy. She had spacious accommodation for 1,200 passengers, in keeping with being originally intended for Oban–Iona–Staffa cruising in the summer and the Gourock–Ardrishaig service in the winter. From 1936 till her retirement in 1969 she was on the Gourock–Dunoon–Rothesay–Tighnabruach–Tarbert–Ardrishaig–Inveraray daily run. This suited me ideally for day-return visits to boats and boatyards in those ports, short of Ardrishaig and Inveraray. She was a congenial ship to travel on, in spite of chronic vibration, and she was much favoured by my sons when they could accompany me during school holidays. Having coffee and hot toast served in style in *Lochfyne's* restaurant was a treat they used to look forward to.

The *Lochiel* at Port Askaig

The other pre-war 'friend' was the *Lochiel*, already mentioned at the beginning of this chapter. A motor passenger/cargo ship built by Denny's in 1939, with a single funnel, one derrick, and, as on the *Lochfyne*, the wheelhouse obstructing the view forward that passengers on the promenade deck might have had. She was on the West Loch Tarbert–Gigha–Islay–Jura–Colonsay run till 1970. To start with, she boasted first and third-class dining saloons and smoke rooms, a first class lounge and first and third-class promenade decks. I have fond recollections of helping Colonsay sheep to embark into *Lochiel*'s tweendecks, up a plank from a small ferry boat, on a dark and early winter's morning. That was before Colonsay acquired a pier.

Of the Caledonian Steam Packet Company's fleet (till the 1973 amalgamation with MacBrayne into CalMac), the ships that have a special place in my memory are the paddle ships *Caledonia* and *Talisman*, the turbine steamer *Queen Mary II* and the post-war *Maids*.

Caledonia, a paddle-steamer built by Denny's in 1934, had a distinguished wartime career as the minesweeper HMS *Goatfell*. Her paddle-box pontoons and her promenade deck formed an excellent auditorium. On one occasion a kilted girls' pipe band from Iowa was performing on the

Caledonia

starboard pontoon. It was watched by a multitude of passengers on that side of the promenade deck and caused the port paddle to be so much out of water that the ship was delayed and nearly missed the tide for disembarkation at Broomielaw.

Leaving the car behind, I took one wife, one dog, five boys, five bicycles and five fishing rods on the *Caledonia* for a true 'doon the wa'er' holiday to Tighnabruaich in the last summer before the 'scenic road' to it from Dunoon was completed.

Caledonia could carry more than 1,700 passengers. I was on her bridge on one evening of the Cowal Games when she came alongside Dunoon pier, thronged with passengers. The radio voice of the traffic manager from the Gourock Office was pressing Captain Donald Crawford to embark at least 2,000. Little did the manager know that the poor captain had a Board of Trade surveyor on the bridge.

Caledonia was sadly sold to a brewery for use as a restaurant on the Thames in 1969. She burnt down in 1980.

Queen Mary II, like *KGV*, was of the second generation of turbine steamers. She was built in 1933 and had, again like *KGV*, the appearance of a miniature cruise liner. She used to leave Bridge Wharf in Glasgow every day at eleven o'clock, calling at Gourock, Dunoon, Rothesay and eventually arriving at Tighnabruaich in the Kyles of Bute at 3 p.m. with Ma, Pa and the weans going 'doon the wa'er'. In the 1950s, at Glasgow

The *Queen Mary II*

Fair time, the shipyards were on holiday for a fortnight, which enabled families to enjoy the Clyde Coast and everyone felt that their holiday had started as soon as they set foot on the steamer. There was accordion music, pipe music and dancing throughout the journey to the coast destination. To celebrate the beginning of the holiday, the father used to announce to the family that he was going down to see the 'engines'. This was his chance to escape down to the bar for a dram. On occasions, when the bar was in full swing, some clever Glaswegian would switch off the bar lights and the barman, in darkness, would shout 'clear the bar', resulting in all glasses being emptied by the culprit before the lighting was restored.

Queen Mary II was much loved by my children and their school friends as the ambience for their birthday parties while cruising. The birthday cakes would be provided by mothers and everything else by the 'Cale' catering department. The little boys were treated with specially put-on deference by the stewards. One little boy, when asked whether everything was to his liking, graciously replied, 'Everything, and I didn't realize that tea with leaves floating on top could taste so delicious!' I last saw *Queen Mary II* at Tilbury in the 1980s, when I was asked to take a look at her with a view to her returning to the Clyde as part of the projected Scottish Maritime Museum. Alas, I found that the restaurant owner who had

The new *Caledonia*

bought her and gone bankrupt had stripped her of anyything that could be sold.

The *Talisman* was unique in being a 'diesel-electric' paddle ship. I remember her particularly as being, at one time, the only conveyance of cars to Millport on the Isle of Cumbrae. They were loaded and unloaded by means of two planks.

The *Maids of . . . Cowal, Bute, Cumbrae* and *Argyll* were convenient motorship-buses in the Firth of Clyde. One of them used to help me get to my Greenock office before anyone else, while at a summer holiday home on Bute. In 1973 the *Maid of Argyll* was sold to a Captain Danielos for service in the Aegean. I had the sad task of preparing her for the voyage, under her own steam, to Piraeus. I asked for all the superstructure windows to be protected by steel plates. A Lamont's assistant manager remonstrated that plywood shutters should do. Captain Danielos corrected him sharply, 'You just do what the surveyor tells you!' Later I discovered that this was one way in which the Captain could import steel plates for future ship-repair work without having to pay duty on them.

The 1970s *Caledonia*, initially on the Ardrossan to Brodick run, was a very different kind of ship from the old *Caledonia*. She started life as a Danish ferry on the short crossing from Copenhagen to Malmö in Sweden.

At least that was her official 'raison d'etre' but in fact she provided a congenial ambience for Swedish gentlemen to enjoy liquid refreshments very much restricted in Sweden. Perhaps that was why she boasted a very elegant saloon. It must have impressed the CalMac purchasing team sufficiently for them not to look into what had to be done to bring the ship up to the UK safety standards.

In the event *Stena Baltica*, or *Caledonia* to be, had to spend many weeks in the Scott-Lithgow's Garvel dry-dock in Greenock. Andy, the manager, daily blamed the Board of Trade surveyor for the delay. As time went on Andy became more and more vituperative on the subject. One day I took the opportunity of being in a huddle of foremen, managers and surveyors to turn to Andy and in a very loud whisper confide that I had a confession to make: 'I have been paid by the Ardrossan Harbour Board to delay the ship until their ferry terminal is ready.'

Andy had a triumphant look on his face: 'There you are gentlemen, something I have always suspected! Surveyors open to bribery and corruption! Wait till the *Scottish Daily Express* hears of this!' Everyone burst out laughing and the now deflated Andy restrained his belligerence somewhat from then on.

Caledonia's long overhaul resulted in Sandy Ferrier, her master to be, and myself becoming good friends, for as long as I had nothing but good to say about Glasgow Rangers. The friendship was hatched while crawling through *Caledonia's* double bottom tanks. Sandy would occasionally join me on Arran to play golf on Ruby's nine-hole course at Lochranza. He would come over with a number five iron over his shoulder announcing that he had been practising drives in the *Caledonia's* wheelhouse. His first drive with that one and only iron would, as often as not, land his ball on the green. Sandy, sadly prematurely departed, was a memorable young character of CalMac's.

The 'MacBrayne' and 'Cale' fleets could boast a good number of memorable characters. John MacCallum, a native of Tiree, chief officer of *King George V*, was outstanding amongst them. He was quite happy with his lot and didn't seem to aspire to a command. One day he was called to the MacBrayne's office in Robertson Street and asked to take command of the wee cargo ship *Loch Frisa* on the morning tide. He turned to the shipping clerk, 'And what do you know about tide mister? Not as much as your wife, she at least knows to put it into washing!'

John liked to draw the passengers' attention to important landmarks on the way from Oban to Iona, 'To starboard is Tiree. Those of you with binoculars will be able to see the smoke from the very active sawmill on the island.'

On seeing the wind rising as *KGV* was ready to leave Tobermory for Iona and Staffa, he would eye the lady tourists and mutter, 'Ay there won't be much powder and lipstick left on them by the time we are round Cailleach Point!'

The barman on *KGV* was very keen to get on the right side of John MacCallum so that he would not be deprived of selling his own stock in the bar. He said to John that there was a dram left for him in the bar by a passenger. John said, 'Is that right?' This happened on five consecutive days, until the barman reminded John that there were now five drams waiting for him in the bar. John once more asked, 'Is that right?' and appeared to do nothing – until the end of the day when he sent down five of his seamen so that they could all have a dram each.

One day, John went down as usual to the saloon for a cup of tea before sailing. He saw a cake which was very tempting and he was about to lift it on to a plate when the chief stewardess shouted 'That will be sixpence Mr MacCallum!' He said 'Well, well, sixpence!' and replaced the cake on the stand. A few weeks later the chief stewardess said to him, 'I've got some friends coming on the cruise today, Mr MacCallum.' John replied, 'No problem, full fare!'

Captain 'Squeaky' Robertson of the *Lochmor* was renowned for his ship repair specifications, such as 'the starboard rail to be bent straight'. When asked by a lady passenger in stormy weather whether his ship was likely to reach her destination, he would say, 'Yes Madam, by the grace of God and Captain Robertson.' He was a stock exchange operator in his own quiet way, having learnt a few tricks of the trade while serving his apprenticeship on large yachts.

Captain MacKinnon, known as 'Polaris' MacKinnon, to distinguish him from at least two other Captains MacKinnon in the company, used to enlighten open-mouthed passengers on the subject of his latest navigational aids, 'I always keep a couple of ducks on the forecastle deck. When I am approaching land I launch them overboard. If they are swimming, I keep on ahead and as soon as they start walking, I go hard astern.'

Captain Dan Sinclair on the *Lochnevis* was known as 'Hurricane Dan'. He got his command late in life and tended to be extremely cautious.

Captain Sandy Campbell, who preceded 'Hurricane' Dan on the *Lochnevis* used to confess to having 'one foot in the grave'. Some years after his retirement I met him on Tiree, hale and hearty and tending his own and another croft.

Captain Dan Macleod of the *Lochiel*, as already mentioned, was a jovial sailor with a distinctive sailor's walk. For many years he courted a lady on one of the islands on his route and when asked why they didn't get spliced, he would say, 'Wait until I retire.' On retirement he promptly married a lady from Crinan. He was followed on the Islay run by the previously mentioned George Smith and later by Sandy Ferguson, who became CalMac's marine superintendent.

Captain John Grey, on *KGV* and later on the *Columba*, had been brought up on Eriskay and was and is an accomplished Gaelic scholar.

Captain Dougie MacCallum on the *Lochfyne* thought it bad luck to have women in the wheelhouse when under way. He used a precise definition for 'a wee dram'. He held that it was half a gill or a tenth of a bottle.

Captain Colin Macdonald was the 'Grand Old Man' of the Western Isles seagoing fraternity. I last saw him, in his retirement, on his native Iona and listened for half a day to his tales of the sea!

Alan Carmichael, 'chippie' on the *Lochiel* was a special friend of mine. After a shipboard accident I went to console him at the Glasgow Southern General Infirmary and spent the whole visit being entertained by Alan with funny stories of his native Port Ellen.

Captain Fergie Murdoch, the last but certainly not the least master of the *Duchess of Hamilton* was another champion at repartee. When a lady passenger complained of a dirty hand towel in the ladies cloakroom, he retorted, 'A thousand ladies used that towel before you, Madam, and you are the first to complain.'

Captain John Cameron on the *QMII* was generally known as Lord Cameron.

Dan MacLean, a native of Tiree, was at one time mate on the *Glen Sannox*. One of his best seamen was transferred to another ship and he was sent a man who was a new start as a replacement. Dan was far from happy with the man's work and phoned the personnel department, 'Where did you find this fellow? Did you pull him out of a lucky bag?'

Angus MacCorquodale, a sailor on the Islay ships, was not very fond of farmers. One such appeared on board his ship with five sheepdogs and asked Angus where to seat them. Angus promptly suggested that he should find five seats for them in the saloon and tie himself to the rail.

Characters they all were, and for all that they didn't take themselves too seriously. They were true sailors to a man and got to their island

John Mackenzie

destinations in all seasons and times of day with the minimum of navigation equipment and guiding lights.

I cannot end my recollection of the seagoing characters of my times without mentioning at least two of MacBrayne's 'captains' ashore.

John Mackenzie was a purser on the old *Lochinvar* and married Flora, Captain Callum Robertson's daughter. He became CalMac's manager at Oban and in that capacity was known as a highland gentleman of charm, good manners and good humour.

Harold Hastie, for many years MacBrayne's agent in Port Ellen, Islay, was of a nautical lineage. His father was the Port Ellen harbourmaster. His mother was a Munro of the Ardrishaig Munroes of Loch Fyne skiffs fame, and his brother Donald was a marine engineer. I remember him as 'King Harold of Islay', but to others he was known as 'Hark the Harold', or 'Harold be thy Name'. By whatever name Harold was known, in his time he probably had as much influence on Islay as the island's laird, who sometimes resided in Islay House.

Harold was involved in just about every activity on Islay, but from childhood he particularly enjoyed messing about in boats. I think he owned

Harold Hastie

one of the ex-Gigha ferryboats, the *Boy Jamie* and the *Happy Return*, the ex-St Catherine's one. Once, over a 'wee sensation', he told me of the wartime occasion when, as a teenager, he was rowing his teenage girlfriend, later Mrs Donnie MacKerral, about Port Ellen harbour. Out of the blue a loud call came from the shore for all Home Guard men to muster as Germans had landed at Kilchiaran. Harold left it with his girlfriend to dispose of the boat and joined the Home Guard detachment boldly marching westwards. It was getting dark when, beyond the Gruinart turning, they sighted a small column approaching from the west. Fortunately no shots were fired before it transpired that the Kilchiaran Home Guard had also been roused, in this case to face the Germans who had reportedly landed at Kildalton.

Mentioning Kilchiaran reminds me of a tale by Kathie Henderson, a native of that Islay township. The ancient Kilchiaran Stone with a Hole, probably an old font, was taken away by a thief in the night. He must have thought better of it because the stone was later found abandoned, but it took six horses to bring it back.

Finally, a reflection on a West Coast ship of an older generation. Capt.

William Robertson, son of Capt. Callum Robertson of the *Lochinvar*, who started his distinguished seagoing career in the 1930s on ss *Hebrides*, was musing about his time on that ship. The *Hebrides* was built in 1898 for MacCallum Orme and was not taken over by MacBrayne until 1948. The crew of that ship was considered amongst the best paid on the West Coast, but they had to be on duty, sometimes for 18 hours a day. It was said that the ship was so popular that there was never a vacancy on her until a sailor disembarked in a coffin.

What made *Hebrides* so attractive, apart from good money, was her reputation as a good training ground for 'blue water' i.e. deep sea service. All that in spite of the crew being convinced that the ship was harbouring a ghost, even if the ghost sometimes turned out to be a sailor having to lean against the rail in the night.

One of the *Hebrides'* masters was John MacKinnon, a crabbed gentleman of Coll. His second mate Donald MacFarlane, another Collach, when approaching Arinagour on Coll moved the telegraph to 'Slow Ahead' before calling the captain, and was promptly rebuked by him. John MacKinnon put the telegraph to 'Full Ahead' and loudly accused the second mate of being afraid of his own island.

Another master of that ship, Dan Macmillan was a congenial man and quick witted. A mature lady passenger took a fancy to him and kept pursuing him with questions. When the ship was heading for Carbost on Skye, she pointed to three sharp peaks and asked why they were called the Three Maidens. 'Because no man ever got on top any of them, Madam' was Dan's reply.

From May until October the *Hebrides* often carried sixty-three cruise passengers for eight to ten days' trips. The cost was £10, which included three meals per day. She called at twenty-six different ports and visited St Kilda at every third trip in the summer. Willie Robertson has a nostalgic memory of some of the Glasgow Orpheus Choir being carried on one of the cruises and of the powerful voices resounding in the wilderness of Loch Skiport at the north of South Uist, where the vessel anchored for the night. The *Hebrides* carried, of course, horses, cattle and sheep and special trips were made during the spring and October sales when full loads of cattle and sheep were taken from the Isles to the Oban or Kyle of Lochalsh railheads. Steerage passengers were carried all year round.

8

A SHORT SPELL ON THE EAST COAST

In 1948 I came to Leith to start working with the Marine Survey Service of what was the Board of Trade, changed to Ministry of War Transport and later became Board of Trade again. It was the time when civil servants' official hours were 10 a.m. to 4 p.m. Needless to say we, marine surveyors, never worked to those hours. They also had six weeks' holidays, rising to eight. Leith was a busy port town, home to several native shipping companies. There was no Forth Road Bridge and we surveyed the Forth ferries, at least one of which was built of iron in the 1870s. There were shipyards in Grangemouth, Burntisland and Leith, and boatyards in Fife and East Lothian, some run by memorable personalities.

Leith of the late 1940s and early '50s, though boasting headquarters of such significant shipping companies as Salvesen's and Currie Line, was very much an olde worlde harbour supporting ship's chandlers, shipping butchers and oil navigation lamp makers. It also had the tiniest of dry-docks, always in use for repairing local coasters. The boss of that modest ship-repairing establishment was wee Mr MacCall whom I never saw without his bowler hat and black suit, and who had his residence in the Royal Forth Yacht Club.

An interesting part of the Port of Leith was the Shore, essentially a quay, stretching from the main dock gate to the Commercial Street Bridge, where Edinburgh's river, the Water of Leith, became salty. Outside the dock gate stood the impressive towered and turreted Sailors' Home, literally home to many seafarers during their spells between ships and to young ships' officers attending nearby Leith Nautical College. There they had comfortable study/bedrooms and enjoyed full Scottish breakfasts, all for 7s. 6d. per night. Their social aspirations were met by weekly dances held in the Sailors' Home and two or three well-frequented pubs on the Shore, the least interesting but most notorious being Rutherford's, affectionately called 'the Jungle' by sailors and locals alike.

The warehouse, emporium and workshop of Messrs M.P. Galloway,

Ships Chandlers, under the management of Mr Niven, just about commanded its part of the Shore. The quayside was always busy, harbouring coastal vessels such as Dennison's *Shapinsay*, which appears in chapter 6, Gibson Rankine's near continental coasters and Danish 'butter and eggs' ships. Across the water stood the grey and melancholy, if classical, edifice of the Custom House and Shipping Office.

The Shore was far from grand, but it had character and the seafaring folk who enlivened it bore a more romantic air than today's bright young things who frequent the 'bistros' into which some of the old buildings have been converted. The Sailors' Home, for instance, now rejoices under the name 'Malmaison Hotel' whose well-heeled patrons would consider it offensive to offer a tip of 7s. 6d., or thirty-seven pence ha'penny in today's money!

Just about the first emergency call I had to answer was one to attend the affectionately named *Cara*, a coal-fired coaster of the Glen shipping company of Glasgow. She was lying on her side at Methil on the coast of Fife, one of the principal coaling ports on the east side of Scotland. The *Cara* had been heading for Preston on the west coast of England with a deck cargo of pit props from the Baltic. She had apparently run into bad weather there and had had to refuel a couple of times before arriving at Methil. At Methil the captain and the chief engineer between them decided to make sure that they didn't run out of coal going north about to Preston. They did that by filling not only the side-bunkers and cross-bunkers, but also the saddleback bunkers, at the sides of and above the stokehold. This bunker stowage was specifically proscribed by the Stability Instructions when carrying deck cargo.

When I arrived on the scene the ship was lying alongside at an angle of about 17° against the quay. When I got on board I had to do a bit of hill climbing to find the captain and the mate sitting on a mess-room bulkhead, each with a glass in his hand. They offered me a cup of coffee, which I took rather amiss as it wasn't coffee they were having in their glasses. Before long, Capt. Cruddace, the marine superintendent, appeared. He saw no danger in the ship carrying on because 'The reserve buoyancy of the deck cargo represented a factor of safety'. In the end we agreed that it wasn't perhaps such a good idea for the ship to proceed on her beam ends.

We adopted a simple trial and error device for getting *Cara* upright for her onward voyage. Having shed a little of the deck cargo, by means of a rope between a bollard ashore and a winch on board, we made her stand up, let go and observed at what angle of heel she settled. This operation was repeated several times until we thought that the ship was stable enough to sail. That was my first, elementary lesson in the nuances of the service.

I was taught another, much harder, lesson only a few weeks later. A call came to carry out at Grangemouth, I think, a safety survey on another steam-powered coaster belonging to John Bruce of Glasgow, but this time oil and not coal-fired. The filling of the boiler oil settling tank in the stokehold was controlled by a float from which a piano wire was led, over a pulley, to a weighted lever closure of the boiler oil pump. I noticed that the float was broken and asked the greaser what, in the circumstances, stopped the pump from overfilling the settling tank. The greaser told me that he did it by simply moving the weight on the lever. At that stage an older Classification Society surveyor intervened by kindly suggesting that I needn't miss my next train to Edinburgh because he would anyway be looking over the stokehold safety plan.

About a week later the news came through that the ship concerned was on fire, and the crew having been rescued, was drifting, ghost like, over the Mediterranean. Apparently the settling tank had been allowed to overflow to the tune of several inches of boiler oil on the stokehold floor. Once in the Mediterranean the oil lying on the hot floor ignited. It took me many years to live down that coaster's fate!

Gibson Rankine Line was a Leith-based company whose coasters traded to near continental ports. Their ships bore Border names, such as *Melrose*, *Dryburgh* and *Heriot*, or from Sir Walter Scott like *Durward*. Being single in those days I used to get myself signed on those ships, for the duration of my holidays, as second mate, at a salary of one shilling per month. Masters and officers of cargo ships in the home trade didn't need to be certificated in those days, although those ships did have to carry certificated able seamen! On the assumption that a Board of Trade surveyor was bound to know a wee bit about navigation a second mate was welcomed on board. It meant 'four-on-eight-off' watches for officers on the bridge, even if only for a few weeks at a time, instead of the 'four-on-four-off' watch routine that was usual in the near continental trade. In practice it didn't always work out that way!

On one occasion, when I was serving on the *Durward*, we ventured to Ghent, via the Ghent canal, which traverses part of Holland before ending up in Belgium. We left Ghent in the evening and although my watch was not due until much later, I stayed on the bridge with the canal

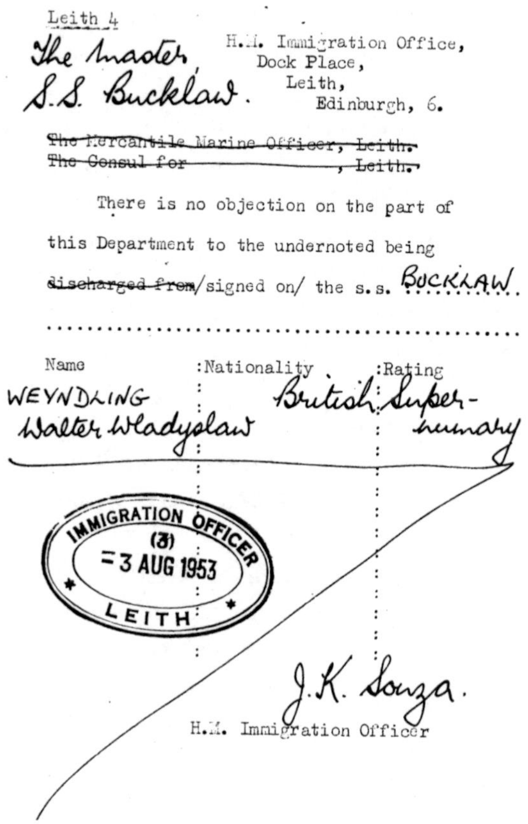

Leith 4

The Master, S.S. Bucklaw.

H.M. Immigration Office,
Dock Place,
Leith,
Edinburgh, 6.

~~The Mercantile Marine Officer, Leith.~~
~~The Consul for , Leith.~~

There is no objection on the part of this Department to the undernoted being ~~discharged from~~/signed on/ the s.s. BUCKLAW.

Name	Nationality	Rating
WEYNDLING Walter Wladyslaw	British	Super-numary

IMMIGRATION OFFICER (3) = 3 AUG 1953 LEITH

J.K. Souza.
H.M. Immigration Officer

Permission to crew on the ss *Bucklaw*

pilot because navigating a busy canal was so interesting. My watch started at midnight and went on till 8 a.m., because the captain was a bit 'tired' that night. The first part of the northward course was quite lively as all the way up to the mouth of the Tyne there were dozens of fishing boat lights to look out for and that was more than enough to keep one awake. Beyond the Tyne the shipping traffic diminished.

The helmsmen, who were experienced ex-trawlermen from Granton, would change on an hourly basis, the spare helmsman brewing tea in the wee water-heating boiler room under the bridge. At the commencement of a wee-sma'-hour's watch the oncoming helmsman noticed me needing matchsticks to keep my eyes open. He made up a little pillow with signal flags and suggested I lean against the bridge bulkhead for an hour's nap, but not before I had given him the course to steer. He repeated after me 'North-by-west-half-west,' and 'As she goes, sir.'

When I was wakened, an hour later, by the change of watch, I heard the off-going helmsman handing over the course 'north-west-by-west-half-west'. The weather was fine and the sea calm but visibility was poor because of 'haar' (the east coast good weather mist) and I leapt to get the radar going. I saw that the ship was heading straight for Bamburgh Castle and suddenly felt the weight of responsibility for the lives of the men trustfully sleeping below. Next there appeared before my mind's eye the day's headline in Edinburgh's *Evening Dispatch* – 'Government Official Wrecks Ship'; or in the *Evening News* – 'Board of Trade Man Puts Ship on Rocks'. I changed the course by four points, just to be on the safe side.

At 8 a.m. the 'haar' had lifted, the sun had come up and the day was smiling at me. The captain ascended the bridge and patted me on the back for having given the Longstone lighthouse a nicely wide berth. For some reason he didn't comment on the fact that the ship was heading north-by-east instead of north-by-west.

On homeward passages from the continent the other ship's officers found it quite useful at times to have a Board of Trade surveyor for their junior colleague. Arriving back in Leith late at night five of us would pile into a taxi. Being the youngest, I'd be expected to sit on top of the luggage facing the other three in the back. Going through customs they would casually draw attention to having the Board of Trade surveyor on board. This, more often than not, resulted in being waved on. Some time later I discovered that I was usually sitting on a large consignment of nylon stockings, which in those early post-war years were worth their weight in gold as presents for wives and sweethearts.

Grangemouth Dockyard remains vividly in my memory, perhaps on account of the larger than life characters I associate with it. Alex Aikman, the managing director, was one of the grand old bosses of Scottish shipbuilding in the mid-twentieth century. He was just as impressive in his forthrightness and decisiveness, as in his human approach and his ability to laugh at himself.

Alex used to tell of how he once dropped into a platers' shed that was rocking with laughter and fell silent as soon as he came in. It took a little arm-twisting to extract from one of the men the story of Alex Aikman being knighted. He was on his knees and the Queen touched his shoulder with the sword and said 'Arise, Sir Alex'. He remained kneeling and the Queen was in the process of repeating the ceremonial when one of the

Advertisement for Grangemouth Dockyard

Grangemouth platers, who happened to be amongst the audience, called out 'He doesn't know what a rise means, your Majesty'. Although never knighted, he did, in fact, receive an OBE.

Alex Aikman was a great raconteur. In his retirement he used to be a fairly frequent visitor in our Glasgow house, because a grandson of his was a school-friend of one of my sons. My mother-in-law, who was quite frail by then and did not often take part in our social life, used to join in whenever Alex Aikman came and she loved to listen to his yarns. He was buried at Kippen and chose the highest point of the churchyard for his grave – to have a view of the hills.

Jimmy Smart was the very true shipyard manager of my era. As I arrived of a morning at his wee office at the Grangemouth Dockyard gate, I was invariably greeted with the bark, 'What the hell is up today?' except when I once came on the morning of 31 December. On that occasion he opened the office safe and disclosed two pretty full bottles. One was marked turpentine and the other paraffin. He took out the bottle containing a liquid in colour vaguely resembling tea, filled the enamelled half-pint mug hanging by a chain from above a stone sink and handed it to me with the command, 'Here you are'. Just as well I didn't have a car in those days!

Whenever I asked Jimmy for a plan relating to the work in hand a cry went forth, 'Boy! Filing system'. The 'boy', whoever he happened to be, then upturned all three table drawers on the office floor, got on his hands and knees, and found the plan asked for. Jimmy Smart might have appeared a rough diamond, but when I had to stay on into the evening, because of an inclining experiment, he drove me home to Edinburgh, to save me waiting for a late train.

The repair manager at the Grangemouth Dockyard was Jimmy Finlay, the same Jimmy Finlay who had been my tutor, boss and friend at the Connell's mould loft at the time of my apprenticeship. He was one of the kindest, humblest and most competent shipbuilders I met during my long association with the industry.

Grangemouth Dockyard was building and repairing a variety of medium-sized and small ships in the late 1940s and '50s. In the early '50s it built two ships for the Halal Shipping Company of Aden, the *El Nabeel* and the *El Nasser*, both of under 300-ft length and of under 2,000 tons deadweight. They were destined for the Red Sea trade, to carry cargo, twelve cabin passengers and an ill-defined number of pilgrim passengers in the 'tween-decks. The passengers' and the officers' accommodation in the bridge and the engineers' cabins in the poop were well in advance of the Red Sea ships of that day. The ships carried a doctor and a two-room hospital in the poop. There was mechanical ventilation throughout the accommodation but no radar. The names of the Halal ships' ports of call sounded as if out of the Arabian Nights' tales or out of a most adventurous travel agency's list: Salalah on the south Arabian coast, Kamaran Island off the Yemen coast, Jedda in Saudi Arabia, Massawa in Eritrea and Berbera in Somalia.

Perhaps the most interesting aspect of the Halal contract was the personality of the owner of that shipping company. Antonin Besse, a Provençal Frenchman, who came to Aden in 1899, and in 1924 had formed his shipping company there. The size of his fleet operating in the Red Sea kept growing and before the Second World War it included some fifteen dhows of up to 400 tons. During the war the RAF stations along the southern shore of the Arabian Peninsula were all fuelled by Besse's dhows.

I met Antonin Besse only once, at the launch of the *El Nabeel* in the summer of 1951. This extraordinary and astute shipowner could be as forthright as Alex Aikman. In his polished speech he assured Alex that he placed his valuable order with the Grangemouth Dockyard only after extensive and searching inquiries into the dockyard's financial stability

Launch of ss *Ajasc* from Burntisland yard

and reliability. Alex Aikman replied in the same vein. Antonin Besse went from the launching of the *El Nabeel* to Gordonstoun and died there. Gordonstoun School was the beneficiary of an annual subsidy from him and the headmaster, Dr Kurt Hahn, was one of his personal friends. Antonin also founded St Anthony's College in Oxford. It was amazing that this Frenchman should have concentrated his European endowments in the UK. Outside Europe he benefited schools in Aden, Arabia, Djibouti and Ethopia. Although a convinced atheist he was ready to help both Christian and Muslim charitable bodies. He was an astounding man.

Burntisland shipyard in Fife was another of my ports of call on the East Coast. I used to visit there once a week, usually by train from the old Caledonian Station in Edinburgh. On a fine summer day I sailed across from Granton, almost opposite Burntisland, in a 14-ft RNSA dinghy, which I had the use of for elementary sailing training on behalf of the local Almond Sailing Club. People I was due to work with in the shipyard, warned of my impending arrival, would look across the Firth and when they could spot a wee sail in the distance would give me about an hour before perhaps calling 'Board of Trade ahoy'.

Miss Victoria Drummond was acting as a shipping company's surveyor, standing by a ship being built at Burntisland. I met her for the first time in the surveyors' changing room and introduced myself. To my acute embarrassment Miss Drummond, a middle-aged lady and holder of a Lloyd's War Medal, stood to attention when she heard the title Board of Trade surveyor. It turned out that she had developed an unhealthy respect for our surveyors since she had been thwarted by them in her numerous attempts at gaining a chief engineer's certificate. Miss Drummond was one of Queen Victoria's god-daughters and from her earliest years was determined to become a marine engineer. This was not regarded as a suitable profession for any woman in the early part of the twentieth century, but for a lady of her background an opening was made in the Holt family's Blue Funnel Line in the hope of it being a girlish whim that would pass in time. It didn't and she was granted a chief engineer's ticket in the end. She was also awarded the MBE and a book has been published about her career and exploits. .

Sir Wilfred Ayre was the boss of Burntisland shipyard in my time. He was, along with his brother Amos, amongst the stalwarts of British shipbuilding between the wars, and after the Second World War. He used to much enjoy having visitors to join him at his pre-lunch aperitif. One of his co-directors used to keep a notebook of personal details of all guests who ever had lunch in their board room. This was the foundation for Sir Wilfred's ability to greet every comer to his pre-lunch drinks with knowledgeable questions relating to his nearest and dearest.

When Sir Wilfred was scraping the barrel for aperitif company, he would send an office boy to seek out the young Board of Trade surveyor in the bowels of a ship under construction and tell him that Sir Wilfred wanted to talk to him urgently. Having rapidly changed out of my boiler suit, I would be invited by Sir Wilfred to help myself to a gin-and-it, which was a trendy drink in those days. To my slight discomfort Sir Wilfred's colleagues tended to peer through the glass door of his office, ready for their lunch, while he was dropping names of show-biz celebrities, such as Beatrice Lilly, he used to meet on Atlantic crossings by *Queen Mary*. Needless to say, I wasn't at my best surveying in the afternoons of a day like that.

When I came to Weatherhead's in Cockenzie, East Lothian, in the late 1940s, they were a well-established boat-building establishment. The

Sir Wilfred Ayre

head of the family, old Sam Weatherhead, was a canny, god-fearing, hardworking Scot and the boatyard was producing a range of sizeable and stout wooden fishing and pleasure boats. The long-lived 46-ft fishing boat *May*, of which much in chapter 3, was one of Weatherhead's products.

An opportunity to get in on the ground floor of the aluminium lifeboat market came about 1950. The demand for ship's lifeboats made of light and easy to maintain material was growing as the post-war boom in Scottish shipbuilding was reaching its peak. The younger Weatherhead generation got quite enthusiastic about diverting the boatyard's resources to the new venture. Lorry loads of structural aluminium alloy, plates and sections, started coming into the yard to keep up ceaseless production but little was done to check the quantities of material delivered. It was suspected that some of it was 'falling off' the lorries on the way, while old Sam Weatherhead scrupulously picked up odd aluminium cuttings to save waste!

The enthusiasm of the younger management and the growth in demand resulted in the Weatherheads expanding the aluminium lifeboat production to two outposts, one in Weatherheads' old boatyard in Eyemouth and the other at Spittal, on the south side of the mouth of the Tweed, already in England. To add to their commitments, Weatherheads took on from Samuel White's, of Cowes Isle of Wight, a subcontract for the construction of aluminium-framed wooden minesweepers for the Admiralty. It seems that the youthful, go-ahead management of the old

Scarlet Cord II

Weatherhead's of Cockenzie

firm had overreached themselves and by 1953 they had to go into voluntary liquidation. An all-night dinner dance was held at a Gullane hotel as a 'thank you' and 'farewell' to all concerned. I believe I was the only invited guest who was neither a redundant employee nor a creditor.

I knew Walter Reekie's boatyard at St Monance in Fife in wartime. Like other boatyards it was busy on Admiralty work and needed an occasional visit from the Naval Construction Department of the Admiralty, in Bath, where I was working towards the end of the war. On one occasion in 1945 my boss, a chief constructor, and I were heading for some shipyards in Aberdeen. On the way we called on St Monance to pay a brief visit to Walter Reekie's boatyard. My boss asked for Mr Reekie and he was pointed out to him as the older chap in a peak cap putting his shoulder to getting a motor fishing boat ready for launching. The chief constructor, very sensibly, didn't want to disturb Mr Reekie and left with an assurance that we would call on the way back from Aberdeen. We did call on the way back and we were faced by Mr Reekie in a top hat, a morning coat and pinstriped trousers. The Chief Constructor was taken aback and feeling apologetic said something like, 'I am sorry to have put you to the trouble for our benefit but I do appreciate your courtesy'. Walter quickly explained, 'I didn't dress up for you man. It's for the funeral I have to attend this afternoon'. Walter, besides being a boat-builder and a saw-miller was also the local undertaker.

Walter Reekie was a natural boat-builder. He was reputed never to rely on construction plans and built his boats by 'rule of thumb'. This meant having a good eye for the shape required, for visualising the proportions needed and being sensitive to the wood material used. He produced many solid and seaworthy fishing boats of the traditional Scottish, double-ended type.

Walter Reekie was an agile and nimble man and didn't spare himself on account of advancing years. In 1950 he killed himself jumping from one fishing boat to another. The word went round that his two sons were not much interested in carrying on the business and that the Reekie enterprises had been left to his daughter. The lady in question was a very attractive young widow. I started to dream about paying court to the beautiful boat-builder's daughter but before I got very far in that direction the word got round and one day I heard my office girls singing: 'She was only a boat-builder's daughter but she gave all her boyfriends a tug.'

INDEX OF BOAT AND SHIPYARDS

INDEX OF VESSELS

INDEX OF PERSONAL NAMES